Family
Tales
from
Tehran

MANIJEH BADIOZAMANI

To Debbie,
a lovely lady.
Enjoy!

Manijeh
Jan. 2020

Mona's Press
3170 Delk Drive
The Villages, FL 32163
FamilyTalesFromTehran@gmail.com

Cover design: GoMyStory.com/John W Prince
Page design: GoMyStory.com/John W Prince
Book production: GoMyStory.com

First edition 2019. Printed in the United States of America.

Library of Congress Control Number: 2018911782

Manijeh Badiozamani

Family Tales from Tehran:
A collection of short stories; a memoir of growing up in Tehran in a house near the Big Bazaar..

ISBN: 978-1-7328561-0-3   EISBN: 978-1-7328561-1-0

Typography
Titles: MB Empire
Text: Caxton Light

The forty-six evocative vignettes in this collection offer the reader a glimpse into an Iran that is rarely portrayed in western literature. They are on the one hand intimate recollections of growing up in and returning to one particular family in Tehran, and on the other hand they offer intriguing perspectives on wider cultural and social norms of Iranian life. An eminently satisfying work that rewards the reader with humor and insight into a place and time that is far away, yet through these stories is still very much approachable. – Dr. Mark David Welton, Professor Emeritus, United States Military Academy at West Point

Family Tales from Tehran is a colorful mosaic of everyday life in Iran's multi-faceted capital city. In the first two sections of the book, Childhood and Grandfather's House; and Relatives and Other Stories, the author, now an American citizen, welcomes us into her childhood home with its neighborhood of shops and markets, and her school, and introduces us to fascinating and sometimes quirky relatives. In the final section of the book, My Trips Back to Iran, Badiozamani details her return to Tehran as she cares for her aging mother. Her stories inform, delight, and provide a bridge between cultures. – Connie Shoemaker, author of *Taste the Sweetness Later, Two Muslim Women in America,* and *The Good Daughter: Secrets, Life Stories and Healing*

Published Stories by Manijeh Badiozamani

Mused Literary Magazine:

http://www.bellaonline.com/review/issues/fall2018/nf008.html *World's Best Key Lime Pie*

http://www.bellaonline.com/review/issues/fall2018/nf003.html *Experience at the Zoo*

http://www.bellaonline.com/review/issues/summer2018/nf002.html *Buying a New House*

http://www.bellaonline.com/review/issues/spring2018/nf006.html *Naneh The Maid*

http://www.bellaonline.com/review/issues/spring2018/nf009.html *The Good Doctor*

http://www.bellaonline.com/review/issues/winter2017/nf003.html *Cream Puffs*

http://www.bellaonline.com/review/issues/fall2017/nf002.html *A Day at the Auction*

http://www.bellaonline.com/review/issues/summer2017/nf001.html *Cousin Shamsi*

http://www.bellaonline.com/review/issues/spring2017/nf004.html *My Mother's Aunt*

http://www.bellaonline.com/review/issues/winter2016/nf003.html *High School Prank*

http://www.bellaonline.com/review/issues/fall2016/nf003.html *Aziz the Story Teller*

http://www.bellaonline.com/review/issues/fall2016/nf005.html *Broken Promises*

http://www.bellaonline.com/review/issues/summer2016/nf001.html *Aziz and the Alley Cat*

http://www.bellaonline.com/review/issues/spring2016/nf001.html *Aziz as My Babysitter*

http://www.bellaonline.com/review/issues/spring2016/nf007.html *Real Argo*

http://www.bellaonline.com/review/issues/winter2015/nf005.html *Play Iranian Style*

http://www.bellaonline.com/review/issues/fall2015/nf002.html *Breaking an Egg*

http://www.bellaonline.com/review/issues/summer2015/nf003.html *Redemption*

http://www.bellaonline.com/review/issues/winter2013/nf002.html *A Marriage Iranian Style*

http://www.bellaonline.com/review/issues/fall2013/nf001.html *At the Airport*

http://www.bellaonline.com/review/issues/summer2012/nf055.html *The Iranian Art of Negotiation*

http://www.bellaonline.com/review/issues/summer2011/nf085.html *My Trip to Iran*

Anthology, The Incredible Shrinking Story; Fast Forward Press 2011

Progenitor Art & Literary Magazine; Volume XLVIII, 2012

Reflections, OLLI South, University of Denver; Volume I, 2016

For

Michael and Eliza

A Different Sort of Life

Table of Contents

Introduction

I'm a first-generation immigrant to America from Iran, having lived in the United States more than fifty years. My grandchildren, who are young adults now, currently have no direct interest in family history, or curiosity about my childhood growing up in Tehran. If someday they do become interested, I might not be around to share with them my memories. This book will help them understand.

Family Tales from Tehran is not a novel. There is no specific plot, or a specific conflict to be resolved at the end. But there are characters and settings. This is a collection of short stories from my point of view and is based on my experiences and recollections as a child—stories about certain life events and encounters with the people around me. The characters are family members and relatives. The setting is Grandfather's house located on Bouzarjomehri Avenue, near the main Bazaar in Tehran, the hub of business and wholesale merchandise.

I have no memory of my paternal grandparents. But when my father was still alive, I asked him to write down his memories of his father—my grandfather. I wanted to know more about the family history, and the family house in which I grew up. My father wrote me a six-page letter and I have incorporated that information in the prologue.

Stories in *Part One* reflect my memories of events that occurred when I was living in Grandfather's big old house. *Part Two* stories are additional memories of relatives and other important people from that time. *Part Three* deals with events that occurred when I went back to Iran for visits.

PROLOGUE

Bits and pieces that I have heard from family members all indicate that my grandmother, Maryam, was a slender, good-looking, religiously devout young woman and the middle girl of three sisters. She was twenty when she had married Grandfather, who was a confirmed bachelor in his early sixties.

At some point in my life, I learned that my grandmother was briefly married to a dashing young officer. The officer had a mistress who was in love with him and jealous of the young bride. No one ever talked about it, and I only learned this, much later, from an old cousin of my father—because I pressed him for information. Reluctantly, he said my grandmother had ended up having a nervous breakdown and the officer divorced her. What a scandalous situation it must have been more than 100 years ago, in that country, for a young woman to be returned to her mother's house! I suppose that might have been the reason she yielded to marry my grandfather who was a lot older, but a well-to-do businessman with a circle of influential friends and a live-in butler. Although I must add that huge age differences were common in Iranian marriages in that society at the time.

The results of this union were two boys, my father, Hassan, and his younger brother by two years, Uncle Jafar.

And that is where the story begins.

Grandfather's property, in the neighborhood of *Sangelaj,* within walking distance to the Big Bazaar on Bouzarjomehri Avenue, was actually two houses adjacent to each other, separated by a wall. I found the original deed to this house among my father's papers. It is a beautiful specimen of penmanship with all the details about the property, signature, and personal stamps, all on a large, gray piece of paper. Although I'm fluent in the Farsi language, I have difficulty reading this document. It is like trying to read and decipher Old Shakespearian English. I have framed this document, which is over 100 years old.

As one entered the property from the street, via a big wooden front door with knockers, one could see a barren courtyard that led to the stable from one side, and to the first building on the other side. This first building was known as *Birooni.* My grandfather used this house to entertain and meet with his friends and business associates. The second house, adjacent to this building was known as *Andarooni* (the inner house). That is where my grandmother lived.

In addition to his wife and two young sons, Hassan and Jafar, Grandfather took care of his mother-in-law, and Grandmother's younger sister, whom we called Aziz. Grandfather apparently maintained a large household until the time of his death. He passed away when my father and Uncle Jafar were young teens.

Grandfather's butler, known as *Agha Baba,* walked the two boys to and from school, and was responsible for shopping and arranging dinner parties in the *Birooni.* I'm told Tehran did not have electricity at that time, so *Agha Baba* would carry a lantern, leading the way, taking the guests home after dinner. *Agha Baba* had left soon after my grandfather passed away. I don't know the reason—and my father did not explain. Either he didn't want to stay on, or my grandmother could not financially afford to have a butler around. I do remember *Agha Baba* visited us occasionally. He was an old man by then, living with his daughter. I liked the mild smell of tobacco on his jacket when he hugged me.

At some point, Grandmother's younger sister, Aziz, had briefly married an old man. He died early in their marriage and left Aziz with a little girl named Homa. They both lived with my grandmother.

After Grandmother passed away, my father moved back into the family house, *Andarooni,* and continued to take care of Aziz and her daughter. I was two years old at the time.

I lived the first twelve years of my life in Grandfather's spacious house with my parents, Uncle Jafar, Aziz and Homa (who was six years older than I), and my younger sister who was born when I was in first grade. My conscious memory begins to kick in when I was roughly four years old.

I've been told that in early days, horse and mules were kept in the stable. But my recollection of that stable is always associated with chicken coops—we had plenty of fresh eggs.

Since we lived in the main house, *Andarooni,* the other house, *Birooni,* was always occupied by, or rented out to, relatives and folks my parents knew. These two houses were separated by a common wall, with a small wooden door which was basically ajar most of the time to allow the occupants to step into each other's courtyard and visit often with ease. The entire wall was covered with honeysuckle. To this day, the fragrance of honeysuckle makes me nostalgic and takes me back to that old place, half-way around the world.

Andarooni had a cellar, a rectangular pool, a big persimmon tree in the middle of the courtyard, and a huge trellis supporting vines which produced big, juicy, light purple-colored grapes, hanging in clusters, and never within my grasp.

I first learned how to dog paddle in the rectangular pool that had greenish-color water. It had a few goldfish here and there. A quick dip in the pool was a cooling mechanism for the hot summer days in Tehran.

I never liked the fruit of persimmon tree. It was eventually chopped down. I could never reach the cluster of grapes, and didn't like them anyway—they had huge seeds inside. Most of the times the neighbors enjoyed the persimmons or the grapes, and showed up with small baskets to harvest.

All the rooms were around the courtyard and some were interconnected. The kitchen and the outdoor lavatory were on the south side of the courtyard, in opposite directions.

Because of the size of the yard, and the big party room called *talaar* on the north side of the house, many wedding receptions were held in our house—weddings of my parents' cousins and other relatives. In those festive occasions, the pool would be covered with a board to create a stage for the musicians and the dancers, appropriately referred to as the "over-the pool entertainers."

The entire six years of my elementary schooling was at a public neighborhood school for girls—tucked away in the back of the Big Bazaar in downtown Tehran. Schools were not co-educational, and I never attended school with boys until I came to the United States when I was 17 years old. I walked to the elementary school daily, meandering through the shops, wholesalers, and vendors in the Big Bazaar.

Uncle Jafar got married when I was ten years old, and his wife joined our household. Thus, eight family members were the permanent residents of our house: my parents, Uncle Jafar and his wife, Aziz and Homa, my younger sister who was born when I was in first grade; and myself.

Part I

Childhood and Grandfather's House

I

The Cellar

The cellar, *zir zamin*, literally meaning underground, was located right below the great room, *talaar,* to the north of the courtyard. The entrance to the cellar was three steps below the courtyard with a low French door. I was scared of the cellar and never dared to go there by myself. To a five-year-old it was dark and spooky, yet fascinating and mysterious. When I was old enough to venture there by myself, I discovered a new and different world in that *zir zamin,* with an abundance of treasures that kept me entertained for hours.

One lightbulb dangling in the middle of the cellar was the only source of artificial light. But there was a long rectangular lattice window above one of the walls which was the source of natural light from outside, and allowed us to have a horizontal view of the courtyard.

The cellar was cool during the summer, but was a bit musty. Sometimes Mother would spread a Persian rug right below the lattice window, with pillows and light sheets, for us to nap in the afternoon while the scorching sun would beat on the bricks in the courtyard.

When my conscious eyes recognized what was in the cellar, I discovered plenty.

Three trunks stood against the wall on one side of the cellar close to the lattice window. Discovering the contents of these trunks not only gave me hours of pleasant fun, but also provided a bit of family history. These trunks belonged to my grandparents, whom I never knew.

Inside the middle trunk were assortments of uncut fabric: silk, cotton, black crepe de Chine, small colorful pillows—all thrown in together.

The trunk on the right contained dishes: mismatched china pieces, platters and bowls of different sizes. My mother referred to these as *Morghi* china—meaning birdlike—because the pieces had birds and flowers painted on them. I'm assuming they were original pieces from China. My mother seldom used them.

But it was the content of the third trunk that I loved the most. This trunk was full of books, many of them leather-bound in brown color. Some were large not only in size, but also large in print. They belonged to my grandfather, which my father had inherited. Digging through this trunk and discovering different books became a hobby of mine as a little girl. Slowly, I learned of the contents. They were mostly on literature, novels, history, and geography.

On the evenings when my father read to us, he used one of these leather-bound books by Alexandre Dumas, *The Count of Monte Cristo*. Homa and I sat on the floor in front of him mesmerized by every word, eager to find out what happened to Edmond Dantes. But of course, my father would stop and leave us hanging until the next evening. No wonder as soon as I learned to read by myself, this book was my constant companion in the cellar in hot summer afternoons in Tehran. This adventure story about hope, justice, vengeance, and forgiveness still remains one of my favorite books! I must have read this book umpteen times both in Farsi and in English!

The cellar contained other stuff, too. Every time I entered this enchanting, yet spooky *zir zamin,* a peculiar pungent smell greeted my nostrils. I was unable to figure out what kind of smell it was. Years later, when I visited the old covered bazaar, this nostalgic smell came back to me.

The combination of leather and spices, entrapped in a cool musty place, was replicated.

At the far end of the cellar, my mother stored food items: huge bins of rice, sacks of dried beans—mostly pinto, kidney and mung beans—as well as sacks of wheat flour that the village head brought us every year from the farm.

Mother also stored sour grape juice in special dark green glass jars with big bellies and long, narrow necks for easy pouring. She used the sour grape juice to flavor soups, *aash*, and stews, *khoresht*. A few containers of honey with honeycomb, jars of homemade cherry and quince jams, which my mother made in season, plus containers of pickles and white cheese were all in the cellar. Different food items such as nuts and dried fruits were stored in bags and were arranged on ledges inside the arches in *zir zamin*.

In the scorching summer afternoons, when the bricks would burn the soles of my feet if I had no shoes on, the cellar was a place of refuge.

2

The Farmland

Grandfather was a landlord and a businessman. He owned several pieces of real estate and half of a small village somewhere near Tehran. By today's standards, the village would have been considered more like a piece of farmland. It was customary for the peasants to work the land and make a living by planting and harvesting. However, they were also required to give a portion of what they had harvested to the landowner; this practice was a remnant of the feudal system. After Grandfather passed away, my father and his brother became the new farmland owners. Somehow, neither of them seemed to be much interested in this inheritance!

My early recollection associated with this inherited farmland is when the Village Head, known as Mash Gharib, came to visit us and brought various food items: sacks of flour, wheat, sun-dried fruits (peaches, apricots, mulberry, and raisins). Sometimes he also brought live chickens. I liked the food from the farmland, particularly the dried fruits and nuts, and the little round flat breads with sesame sprinkled on top and baked in the village clay oven.

My parents didn't seem pleased by and didn't look forward to the visits by Mash Gharib. My father and Uncle Jafar always gave the impression that they preferred not to receive anything and thus not to be bothered by the visits. I never knew how large the farmland was, or its exact location, or the circumstances of their ownership. Simply because they never talked about it.

When Mash Gharib came to visit, he was never alone. He brought along his wife and several of his children. Invariably, a couple of them had health issues. It was expected of the land owner, meaning my father and Uncle Jafar, to take care of the ailments of these peasants. Health issues ranged from the wife's "female" problems to their children's pink eyes.

Uncle Jafar was not married at the time and was never interested or willing to deal with these issues. Thus, it was my parents' responsibility to take care of the visiting folks from the village. And it was my mother who took them to the hospital, arranged for the necessary medication, housed, and fed them for the duration of their stay in Tehran.

Mash Gharib was a short, muscular man with tanned and weather-beaten skin. He was a jolly fellow, as I recall. He talked loudly and smiled broadly as he spoke, which made his saliva sprinkle all over the place. Since he was from the village, he had a peculiar accent. Whenever he showed up at our door hauling sacks of goodies, he created an interesting and fun spectacle for all to watch. He always wore baggy pants held by elastic at the waist and around the ankles. His cloth-woven slippers with hard soles *(geeveh)* were typical peasant attire, distinctly different from the city dwellers. Mash Gharib also smoked a pipe with a long tube. My mother despised his smoking and complained to my father: "These peasants dump their tobacco in the corner of the guest room or under the Persian rug," I heard her say to my father.

I think if my father and his brother had a choice of relinquishing their responsibilities as landlords, they would have preferred to give up the farmland all together.

Mash Gharib brought plenty of flour which Naneh, the maid, used for making noodles and bread. Naneh's special talent was to use the flour to make flat, round, slightly sweetened bread. I loved to watch her while she prepared the dough at home in a huge tub. Afterwards she would put the tub over her head and walked to the local bakery, about a block from our house.

We didn't have an oven at home, and my mother never baked. They had a special arrangement with the local baker. Many times I wanted to accompany Naneh to the bakery, but was not allowed to do so. Naneh usually stayed at the bakery until all the dough was baked into rounds with sesame seed sprinkled on top. The bread was delicious for breakfast with butter and jam and a glass of tea. Or we ate it as snack.

As the years went by, towards the end of my elementary school years, the offerings and the visits by Mash Gharib dwindled. However, there were no complaints from my parents regarding the lack of visitors from the farmland, it was as if it were a piece of forgotten property.

Then the Shah of Iran initiated his White Revolution aimed at social reform. On top of the Shah's agenda was the distribution and release of farmlands by the land owners to the farmers. The intent of the Land Reform was to give the farmland to the folks who actually worked it. The Shah wanted to do away with the feudal system of the past and modernize the country. This was a sweet and welcome reform and what my father and his brother had been waiting for.

Hassan and Jafar were delighted to relinquish their ownership and let Mash Gharib take over the land. After that, we never saw or heard from the Village Head and no one in the house ever spoke of the farmland again.

3

Naneh the Maid

My mother and her younger sister, Aunt Ashraf, had a falling out when I was in elementary school. Naneh, the maid, appeared to be the culprit.

Naneh was Aunt Ashraf's maid. I don't exactly know where she came from or who had recommended her as a maid to my aunt. I perceived her as old at the time, but Naneh must have been only in her early forties.

Naneh was short, barely four feet tall. She was tiny and always wore a head kerchief with some of her fuzzy salt and pepper hair sticking out on the sides, right above her ears. She was somewhat funny-looking, particularly when she smiled. She had only two large teeth in her mouth: one tooth on the upper gum, the other slightly off center on her lower gum! Naneh spoke Turkish that makes me believe she must have come from a Turkish-speaking province in Iran. She also spoke some Farsi with a heavy Turkish accent, which enabled her to communicate with us. Naneh was very quick, and moved about the house swiftly and with agility. It was said she had two grown daughters somewhere in Tehran, but I never saw them. My aunt, who had several small children at the time, along with an irascible husband, seemed to enjoy Naneh's company when she lived with them in their big house.

Two or three times a month, we dropped in to visit Aunt Ashraf. Naneh always served tea, fruit, and cookies. On certain occasions, she made popcorn for us kids. Popcorn in the Farsi language is referred to as *Chose Feel,* which literally means "elephant's fart." So there was a lot of giggling and laughing going on as we ate the "elephant's fart" that Naneh served in a big bowl. Naneh lived in Aunt Ashraf's house for several years, and then suddenly one day she just packed her bag and came to our house!

I came home from school one afternoon and found Naneh standing in the middle of the courtyard, speaking loudly in broken Farsi, declaring she will never go back to "that household" (meaning my aunt's house), and that if my parents did not keep her, she would go and sleep on the street corner! She probably used it as a threat, since my parents would have never allowed Naneh to be a homeless person. I don't recall the circumstances that led to Naneh leaving my aunt's employment and coming to our house. We already had a full house: my parents; Uncle Jafar and his wife; my father's widowed aunt, Aziz, along with her daughter, Homa; myself; and my three-year old younger sister—we all lived together in Grandfather's big old house. But Naneh had definitely declared her intention to join our household.

Naneh's move caused a difficult situation for my parents and put a strain on the relationship between my mother and her younger sister. No amount of reasoning would persuade Naneh to go back. At the same time, my parents felt sorry for Naneh and wanted to provide her with a shelter. They agreed to keep her temporarily until she and my aunt had calmed down. Their decision created a huge family feud between the two sisters. Aunt Ashraf accused my mother of stealing her maid. I don't know all that was said between them because grownup business was seldom discussed in front of the children. However, the end results were that Naneh stayed and we stopped visiting Aunt Ashraf for a very long time.

Naneh swept the floors, washed clothes and dishes, and helped with the chores around the house. She never did any cooking because my father never accepted anyone else's cooking except my mother's. Aziz was in charge of daily shopping. So Naneh's role was limited to household chores, but with one exception, and that is when she took it upon herself to bake bread, utilizing the flour brought to us from the farmland that was stored in the cellar.

Naneh smoked several times during the day, usually after she was done with a chore. There was a ritual to her smoking, and I liked to watch her as she rolled her own cigarettes. She had a small pouch of tobacco, and a small box where she kept her cigarette papers. She would take a little tobacco from the pouch, put it in the center of a very thin paper, then roll it and lick one side of the paper with her tongue sticking out, which exposed her bottom tooth. She then put the rolled cigarette in a cigarette holder, leaned back against a wall in the courtyard, and enjoyed her puffs.

Whether or not she really enjoyed being part of our household, which was a lot more structured and disciplined than Aunt Ashraf's house, I will never know. I'm not sure whom she considered to be her boss: my mother, my father, or Uncle Jafar? Certainly she did not want to take orders from Aziz or Uncle Jafar's wife.

Just as she had left Aunt Ashraf's house without warning, Naneh packed her bag one day and left us. This time she moved to the house of my mother's cousin. By eavesdropping on grownup conversation, I learned that Naneh had left us claiming "there were just too many people in that house," which was the truth.

By then, Naneh's move did not come as a surprise. Her behavior was well analyzed by the adults in the family and no one took offense that she had left us abruptly. My parents handled Naneh's departure casually, and it did not cause any friction between my mother and her cousin. Naneh's sudden departure, however, did not ease the tension between my mother and her sister. They seldom spoke to each other till the end!

When Naneh left us, my mother's cousin was a newlywed. That explained Naneh's smart move. It made sense to her to join a family where she thought the workload would be less. After a few years in the employment of Mother's cousin, Naneh went back to her village in the Turkish province where she was from and didn't come back to Tehran again.

In her own way, Naneh had created adventure and excitement in her life. She had travelled to the big capital city of Tehran, had experienced living in comfortable homes, had earned some money, and then had returned to her village for good.

4

Naneh and Mash Gharib

Mother told me this story about Naneh and Mash Gharib (the Village Head from the farmland).

The big and spacious courtyard in Grandfather's house was the site of many wedding receptions. Neighbors and relatives usually used our house for such festive occasions. One such reception was when my mother's cousin, Ismail, married a pretty girl named Tooba.

The rectangular pool played an important role in becoming a makeshift stage for entertainment. A thick board would be hauled in to cover the pool, and a large Persian rug would be spread to cover the board. It was fun and exciting to have a group of singers, dancers, and musicians perform in our yard on this mini stage. Neighbors usually climbed on top of their roof tops, walked on the roof of our house, or perched on top of the wall between the houses to watch the entertainment. These entertainers were aptly called *Motreb Rou Hozie*, which literally means "musicians who played over the pool."

The ritual of getting the yard ready for the reception created a lot of commotion, traffic, noise, and excitement in the house. Rented chairs and small tables were hauled in and arranged around the stage and over the entire courtyard. Each table had on it the customary platter of cookies and pastries, a separate bowl for fresh fruit, an ashtray with a match box inside, and a few small plates. Special chairs were reserved for the bride and groom close to the covered pool. Old and young mingled, talked, and laughed. Children roamed around while the musicians played and sang, and the dancer danced in colorful costumes. The dancer, who held a tambourine while wiggling her body to the sound of the *tar* (string instrument) changed costumes periodically. These entertainers were not expensive to hire, and always were available at short notice.

It so happened that this festive occasion coincided with one of Mash Gharib's visit to Tehran. Since he stayed at our house, he was intrigued by all the excitement and the commotion of getting the courtyard ready for the wedding reception. He was a peasant from the village and was in awe of all the preparation done by the city folks.

As told by my mother, Mash Gharib decided to extend his visit in order to experience a city wedding reception. He stayed out of sight, half-hidden in one of the rooms around the courtyard, and watched the guests, in their party attire, and the entertainers through a window. It must have been quite a show for him.

The party continued through the early hours of the morning. Mash Gharib, who was not used to staying up so late, somehow fell asleep in that room in the dark. Apparently, that was the room where Naneh frequently used to stretch or take naps. Being very late, and while the party was still going on, Naneh—without turning the light on—slipped into the room and fell asleep besides Mash Gharib, unknowingly (that is what Mother said) resting her head on his stomach!

Whatever caused Naneh to wake up in the middle of the night is not known to me, but the story has it that there was a loud shrill from Naneh, which in turn was followed by a scream from Mash Gharib, who was equally frightened, and started yelling his head off.

Mother did not tell me the rest of the story, but having seen both Naneh and Mash Gharib, I find it absolutely hilarious when I visualize this episode.

5

Aziz as My Babysitter

As far back as my memory registers, Aziz, my father's old aunt, lived with us in Grandfather's house.

Aziz helped with a variety of chores and household duties. She shopped daily for bread, meat, vegetables, and dairy products. She also helped my mother in the kitchen. Our house was a short distance from the *Bazaarche,* the little bazaar. Sometimes I pestered her to take me along, but she knew I would slow her down and preferred to go alone.

In addition to her daily chores and the ritual of breaking an egg when I was sick (a ritual designed to identify the culprit who made me sick, as described in another story), Aziz also served as my babysitter. When I began to understand that my parents left me at home with Aziz to go out and have fun, I would start fussing and throwing tantrums.

At the age of five, my resentment and the tantrums took a truly serious turn. How dare they go out without me!

On those occasions when I was determined to throw a tantrum in order to get my way, Mother casually would ask me to run an errand for her:

"Would you go to Aziz and bring back my special box?"

"What special box?" I would ask with a tinge of curiosity.

"Oh, ask her for my Sitandhold box. She borrowed it last week and hasn't returned it yet," Mother would reply. "Do tell her I need it urgently."

With brisk, quick steps I would run over to Aziz's room, located at the other end of the courtyard.

"My mom wants her Sitandhold box immediately," I would demand, with a tinge of childish arrogance and authority.

Aziz would scratch her head, pretend she was thinking, and then she would say:

"Come on inside. I have it somewhere here. Let me look for it."

She would smile and let me into her room. More than ever, I would be curious and anxious to see this special box.

Aziz would start pulling out drawers of her tiny dresser. No box there!

She would search under the bed, and quietly mumble:

"Whatever happened to the Sitandhold box."

She would talk to herself and I would listen carefully to find out where she would search next.

The pantry adjacent to her room had a curtain drawn in front of it. I was not allowed to go in there—and frankly I didn't have any desire to enter it either. It was dark and spooky.

Aziz would disappear in the dark pantry, still talking to herself and making noise. While I patiently waited for her, I would see an assortment of interesting stuff—toys and pieces of clothing that had spilled out of her drawer onto the floor while she was looking for my mother's special box. I would sit down and start examining those interesting items while Aziz was still in the pantry.

It wasn't until much later in life that suddenly I recognized the significance and function of the *Sit and Hold Box.*

6

Aziz the Storyteller

Throwing tantrums when my parents left me with Aziz was my normal routine. But as I got older, Aziz used her story-telling techniques to keep me occupied. We had no children's books in the house. The leather-bound books that were kept in the *zir zamin*, the cellar, or the ones that my father read to us were mostly for grownups. No wonder the very first novel my father read to me was *The Count of Monte Cristo,* by Alexandre Dumas.

But Aziz had all these stories in her head. Her fascinating tales kept me mesmerized. I could sit quietly and listen to her attentively for hours. That is exactly what she wanted—to keep me quiet and entertained.

Aziz was a devout Muslim and her stories had religious backgrounds and undertones, though I didn't know it at the time. From Aziz I heard, for the first time, about God, Adam, and Eve; heaven and hell; the forbidden apple tree in paradise; and a vicious and double-crossing serpent. I heard about a boy who did not do as God told him and was swallowed by a great big fish. No worries, she would say, the boy came out unharmed and followed God's commands. She told me about a prophet who parted the sea and that he could turn his staff into a snake. I learned about Noah and the flood and the ship Noah built and all the animals in it. I also learned about a prophet who was asked to sacrifice his own son for God. But she would hastily emphasize that God spared the son—it was just a test of loyalty! And many more stories.

As a good Muslim, Aziz opted to wear a *chador* to cover herself when she left the house, she never missed a prayer, and she always fasted during the month of Ramadan. She was a bit on the fanatic side. Aziz was a good person, but she and my father sometimes clashed bitterly on ideas and plans for Homa's education. Homa was Aziz's only child. Such clashes came to a head when my father insisted that Homa had to continue her education and become a teacher, but Aziz wanted to keep her daughter at home! Of course, my father won—he always did!

Homa went on to become an excellent math teacher and later on won citations from the ministry of education for the work she had done. Homa became financially independent and was able to take care of Aziz in her old age. My cousins were the recipients of Homa's mathematical talents when she tutored them off and on, but by then I had already left Iran and was living in the United States.

When my son was born he received, as a gift, a Bible Story book for children. Night after night, as I read those short stories to him, I realized I had already heard them all from Aziz. Yes, the book of Genesis in the Bible is similar to the story of creation in the Quran. Aziz, by telling stories, was teaching me about the creation.

Yet Aziz was very superstitious and believed in the hidden meaning of certain events in life. It was funny and annoying at the same time when we were getting ready to leave the house and someone would sneeze—Aziz would make us all wait for a few minutes before leaving. If she spilled a glass of water, which she often did, she would comment: "Spilled water brings light into life." If bird droppings fell on our head or clothes, she firmly believed it was good luck, and that fame and fortune were awaiting us.

When any of us got sick, whether we had a common cold or fever, or even something more serious, Aziz believed it was due to "evil eyes." She would say someone—family member, friend, or neighbor—had cast an evil eye, and that the only way to identify that person would be by "breaking an egg."

7

Breaking an Egg

I am sick in bed, another bad case of tonsillitis. I'm feverish and my throat hurts. Aziz believes that the evil eyes of a relative has caused my sickness. She can find out whose eyes it was by breaking an egg!

The ritual begins, and I'm so absorbed concentrating on what she does that I forget about my fever and sore throat. First, she spreads a square handkerchief open. She then pours some table salt in the middle of the handkerchief. Meticulously she places a coin on top of the salt.

Then she takes a medium-sized raw egg between her thumb and index finger. While holding the egg, she utters loudly the names of the people I came in contact with before I got sick. After uttering each name, she draws a tiny line on the egg with a small piece of charcoal—the names of the people I came in contact with before I got sick:

"Khaleh joon," my mother's widowed aunt.

"Esmail Agha," Khaleh joon's twenty-year-old son.

"Uncle Jafar," my father's younger brother.

"Naneh," our old maid.

"Sadegh Khan," my father's cousin.

And, after a short halt, she decides to add a line for Sadegh's wife as well.

She even includes my mother and father—two lines for them—but she never mentions herself. Aziz rattles off some more names, and the white egg is marked with short black lines all over.

Very carefully, she puts the marked egg on top of the coin and gathers the corners of the handkerchief around the egg. Holding the covered egg in the palm of both hands, she then begins repeating each name all over again while giving a gentle squeeze to the egg after each name. At some point the egg, which is rubbing against the coin, breaks at the mention of a name. Aha, that is the person with the evil eyes!

Since I get tonsillitis quite often, Aziz breaks many eggs for me. I love this ritual; like magic it makes me forget about my sickness! Amazingly, each time, a new individual is the cause of the inflammation of my tonsils! Sometimes she goes on for a long while, repeating all the names before she finds the culprit. Other times, and it seldom happens, the mention of the first name causes the egg to break. In this particular instance, it is Esmail Agha, the son of my mother's widowed aunt who is the guilty party.

She gives the coin to a beggar in the street, throws away the broken raw egg, and cleans the handkerchief for the next time I get sick. It is comforting to blame my frequent tonsillitis on others! Along with Aziz's discovery, a nurse comes to the house and gives me injections of penicillin and Vitamin C.

Finally, at the age of twelve when I have my tonsils out, Aziz stops breaking eggs for me.

8

Aziz and the Albino Cat

When I was six, I saw a calico cat turn albino. I saw it with my own two eyes.

Alley cats were common visitors at Grandfather's house. They arrived at odd hours and left as they pleased. They roamed around the courtyard, lingered by the rectangular pool, and drooled over a few goldfish that were oblivious to the nearby danger. Sometimes, these stray cats perched quietly on the brick wall that separated houses.

Often they explored the roofs, jumping from one to another, and at times fought and growled at each other—God knows over what. These gypsy cats never stayed in one place. Certainly they were not invited to come inside the rooms of the house. It was absolutely prohibited.

If I saw a visiting cat getting close to the pool, I imitated Aziz by stomping my feet down and waving my hands, dismissing the cat while loudly yelling *"Peesht."* That would scare the cat—it would jump over the wall and into the neighbor's courtyard. The neighbor then had to decide what to do with the new visitor.

But once a plump calico cat did not want to leave our courtyard and lingered for days and weeks. Aziz kept saying *"Peesht"* and even once threw a shoe at it. Still the cat did not budge. That prompted Aziz to devise a plan of action.

She grabbed a big burlap sack from the cellar—the flour sacks that Mash Gharib, the farmer, had brought from the village. We had plenty of those in the cellar. The sack still had some flour left in it, but Aziz didn't care. She put some delicacy that cats like to eat inside the sack and left its top open. She put the sack in the yard, near her room. Then she kept watch from her window. The greedy cat found its way inside the sack and while it was busy chewing on the delicious morsel, Aziz ran to the yard, grabbed it, pulled the draw strings, and tied the top of the sack.

The cat growled, kicked, and pushed. But Aziz did not give in. I didn't know what she was going to do with this bundle of joy. Cats are smart and Aziz knew if she let the cat out several blocks from the house, it would find its way back. But Aziz was smarter than the cat.

She put on her *chador* and grabbed the sack, with the cat still growling and fighting to get out. With Homa and me in tow, she led the way to the nearest bus stop. She paid the fare and instructed us to move all the way to the back of the bus.

Suddenly the cat was silent. Maybe it was trying to figure out what was happening or where we were going. But its vigorous moving inside the sack continued. This made Aziz's *chador* sway left and right, back and forth. Homa started giggling and I followed suit, but Aziz frowned and told us to be quiet! A few passengers sat in front of the bus and no one paid any attention to the back row. We were on that bus for a long time until it reached the end of its route. That was the destination Aziz had in mind.

We got off the bus in a part of the city I had never seen before: a new subdivision, sparse houses, and plenty of land. Still Aziz made us walk for a while. Then she stopped at the corner of an empty lot.

Slowly, she opened her *chador* and put the sack down. Gingerly, using extreme caution, she untied the drawstring while holding the sack away from herself and loosened the top. As soon as the sack opened, the prisoner, who had kept quiet and still, darted out in a flash and ran without looking back. It was not the same calico cat, but an albino—a white creature from head to the end of its tail.

9

Early Education

When I was four, I had a brief and unsuccessful encounter with something my parents called "kindergarten." I have no idea how long I attended—perhaps a week or two—and then they stopped sending me. I have only one memory from this period.

The private kindergarten was owned by a husband and wife team. The husband was known as *Baba Noghli,* "candy man." At the end of each week, he would hand the kids a little bag of *Noghl,* candy-coated slivered almonds.

On the days I attended, Mother sent me prepared; she braided my long hair and attached a ribbon at the end of each braid. She fixed me a snack bag—I had no idea what was in it—and then I waited for a van to come and pick me up.

It was snack time at the kindergarten. The teachers read the names of each child written on the bags and handed out the snacks. They held up a bag and called a name: "Golbabai" (my last name).

Nobody raised a hand. She said it clearly and louder a second time: "Golbabai." No response. A few kids started looking around to see if there was someone by that last name. So did I! Repeating after some other kids, I also asked, "Who is Golbabai?"

Whether I was too young for the experience, or too dumb to even know my own last name, or too shy, the end result was that I did not go back to kindergarten—or was it a pre-school?

A couple of years after the "kindergarten" episode, I was most eager to start first grade. Pourandokht Elementary School for girls was smack in the middle of the Big Bazaar in Tehran.

The Bazaar was the major business district in Tehran, and I had to walk several blocks—passing by the stores of the wholesale merchants, hearing the loud noise of street vendors, avoiding the pedestrian shoppers and donkeys loaded with cargo, and crossing a very busy traffic intersection. There was no other way to get to school, actually that was the shortcut.

Homa, my father's cousin, was a sixth grader in that school when I began the first grade.

On my first day of school, at the age of six, I was entrusted to Homa to help me cross the busy intersection and guide me to school. I was instructed to come back with her when we were dismissed for lunch.

As recounted by my mother, around noon she saw me bounce into the house with loose braids, ribbons missing, rosy cheeks, uniform half-unbuttoned, laughing, and announcing,

"I came back all by myself."

They must have been mortified! It wasn't just the distance that worried them, but also crossing the busy traffic intersection and the crowds in that labyrinth of shops and wholesalers. To find one's way through the Bazaar required knowledge of the place, and a six-year-old was not supposed to walk there alone. But I did!

If Homa was chastised for letting me out of her sight, I didn't know. But it certainly gave me a sense of independence and accomplishment for the rest of the year, even though I was under strict orders to walk to and from school with Homa.

Bittersweet memories of the first grade weren't just confined to walking under the watchful eyes of Homa, it had also something to do with my first-grade teacher.

Miss Motalebi was short, fat, and had a round face with a dark complexion. She was not married, and I had heard Aunt Tooran, who was also a teacher in another elementary school, refer to her as "that round radish." I had no idea what that meant. But I loved school in general and adored Miss Motalebi, in particular.

With childish eagerness to please my teacher and to let her know that I liked her, I took some hard candies to school one day. Though we were not supposed to enter the classroom until the bell rang, I walked in and arranged the candies neatly on her desk.

I was beaming with happiness and my heart was beating with excitement. I could hardly wait for her to discover the candies and thank the person who had put them on her desk.

We sat in our designated seats, and Miss Motalebi walked in and sat in her chair behind her wooden desk. Suddenly she spotted the candies. With a disgusted tone of voice which expressed her intense loathing, and with anger in her eyes, she yelled,

"Who the hell put these on my desk?"

Without hesitation, still wanting to be acknowledged for something nice I had done for my teacher, I raised my hand. She then quickly added,

"Come right away and remove these candies and don't you ever do that again!"

Something tiny inside me died at that moment. I was embarrassed and heart-broken. I got up and walked to her desk, picked up the candies, and stuffed them into my uniform pocket.

10

A New Sister and Cream Puffs

A keen memory is the birth of my sister, who was born when I was in the first grade. In the morning, when Mother went into labor, my father hurriedly took me to a neighbor's house to have breakfast, and then off to school I went with Homa.

Oblivious to the events in my house, I came home from school and, voilà, there was a new baby! For the next few days, a steady stream of relatives, neighbors, and friends stopped by to congratulate my parents and brought the customary baby gifts: flowers, toys, and sometimes boxes of pastries.

One of my aunts showed up with a huge box of pastries from a well-known patisserie. My father immediately opened the box and passed it around the room where several relatives, anticipating the box would be opened, carefully followed it with their eyes. As a short, six-year-old kid, I kept stretching my neck to see what was in the box to decide which of the pastries I wanted to have.

A perfectly round cream puff, with a bit of custard oozing out from the side and dusted with powdered sugar, was elegantly nestled in a white muffin paper cup. That was the one I wanted. But it was not my turn yet, I had to wait until the box reached me. I prayed no one would take it.

With transfixed eyes on the box, and anxiety in my belly, I followed its movement around the room. Now there was only one person between me and the box, and that was Homa. She got hold of the box and went straight for the cream puff. I raised my voice in objection:

"But that is the one I want."

I was almost ready to cry.

Homa was holding the pastry in her hand. But, as soon as I declared my intention, she shoved the whole thing into her mouth and with puffy cheeks gave me a calm sideways glance.

I held back the tears—it was neither the time nor the place to throw a tantrum over a piece of pastry that had already been swallowed. The trauma of being deprived of that cream puff left its mark and I was scarred for life!

Amazingly, we all survive the traumas of childhood, but of course never forget them!

‖

Broken Promises

Riding on the choo-choo train that took us to the southern part of Tehran for an outing in the country was exciting. I was five years old when I first rode the choo-choo and fell in love with the open-air carts, wooden seats, and the smoke from the train engine, as well as the sound of the long whistle. But the most enjoyable part of the trip was the papier-mâche doll my parents bought me at the train station. It was the first doll I owned, but it didn't last long and after a couple of days it fell apart.

When I was six and in the first grade, Uncle Jafar promised to buy me a pretty doll if I ranked at the top of my class. The year ended and I brought home my report card. I had all A's and ranked first in my class. But there was no sign of a doll anywhere in the house. The disappointment was unbearable, so I confronted Uncle Jafar,

"Where is my doll?" I demanded.

He didn't like my attitude and the questioning tone of my voice. But I felt entitled—I had brought home an excellent report card and wanted the promised doll.

Uncle Jafar raised his eyebrows, and then frowned, his thick brows knotting together,

"Maybe later," he said.

I wanted my doll right at that moment, so I made a pest of myself by repeating my demand over and over again. Uncle Jafar was irritated, my mother felt utterly embarrassed, and my father boiled with anger. But I kept whining and bugging Uncle Jafar—and then threw my customary tantrum! It was perfectly logical to demand the prize I was promised.

Uncle Jafar had an appointment. He gave me a nasty sideways glance. Without saying a word, he headed toward the front door and out into the street. My little brain dictated I was entitled to collect my prize because I had kept my part of the bargain. Why wasn't he willing to drop everything and get me the doll?

I ran through the courtyard and followed him outside, sobbing and screaming. At this point my parents' patience wore out completely. I was yanked into the house and given a good spanking. Surely, there was no justice in this world. Why was I being punished for doing well in school and getting good grades? I didn't understand grownup logic and behavior.

Three days passed. Then Uncle Jafar handed me a pretty little doll with golden hair and blue eyes that opened and closed when I tilted its head. The joy of getting a doll was mitigated by the agony of my previous punishment. I simply and quietly said thank you.

When I was in third grade, Aunt Mary, Uncle Razmi's wife, announced she was making me a doll. Wow, a hand-made doll! What a treat. *Norouz,* the Persian New Year when adults are supposed to give children presents, was coming up. Aunt Mary didn't have anything for me, but she was making me a doll. It wasn't finished yet. I could wait.

Two months passed by and there was no sign of the doll. I was playing with Aunt Mary's niece one afternoon. I mustered enough courage to ask her to check and see if the doll was finished yet. She came back and reported the doll was almost finished and that Aunt Mary was planning to hand it to me herself along with some cash, as a late *Norouz* present.

Almost a year went by and still there was no sign of the doll. By then I was older and wise enough to realize not all grownup promises will be kept.

12

Cousin Shamsi

My mother's older brother, Gholam, had divorced his wife. According to family gossip, his ex-wife was a good-looking, ill-tempered, feisty, spoiled, and conceited shrew who constantly fought with Gholam and the rest of the family. The marriage had ended in divorce. She had packed up and taken with her almost everything there was in the house. However, she had left behind their two children: a six-year-old daughter named Shamsi, and a four-year-old son, Hossein. Shamsi was seven months younger than I. A few years after the divorce, Gholam had remarried, but, unfortunately, Shamsi and the stepmother did not get along and another family hell was created for Uncle Gholam.

Shamsi had inherited her mother's good-looks, ill-temper, and foul mouth. I didn't care for Shamsi at all, but tolerated her in the family gatherings. I disliked her selfishness and feisty nature! What I detested the most was how the grownups catered to Shamsi and excused her bad behavior due to the fact she was deprived of motherly love and had a stepmother. Apparently, everyone remembered the story of Cinderella and the wicked stepmother! I didn't like her because she was good-looking, flirtatious, arrogant, and aggressive.

During those summers when Shamsi would come to stay at our house, I knew I was going to have a miserable time. She was not an easy-going person, and her bad temper always landed us in arguments and fights. Uncle Gholam traveled and was on the road a lot. So to keep peace on his home front, he would bring Shamsi to our house, hand her a wad of cash, and leave her under my parents' care and supervision. No one ever asked me if I wanted to have Shamsi as a playmate! I guess we both felt a tinge of jealousy towards each other—she was jealous of my family situation, and I was jealous of her carefree and wild spirit, which did not seem to get her into trouble with my parents. We definitely did not get along and were two different types of peas in different pods. Coming to our house was a respite for Shamsi and my parents were well aware of it, but it certainly ruined many of my summer vacations.

"Obedience" was the name of the game with my parents. I knew that if I was not in compliance with the rules they set, there would be consequences. So it was very disturbing to witness how Shamsi did not have to obey the rules in my house. If her behavior was unacceptable to my parents, she was not punished because she was a guest. I hated my parents' double standards. I was supposed to be ladylike whereas Shamsi was free to be flirtatious, behave as she pleased, and—with the wad of cash her father gave her—she could spend as much as she wanted, on anything she liked.

I also resented the sense of pity and sympathy that she invoked in the grownups. I don't know how harsh or unkind her stepmother was towards her, but in my own mind I had no doubt that Shamsi, with her foul mouth and bad temper, contributed to the situation. Whatever the circumstances, it must have been really bad because she eventually ran away from home in her late teens.

In the past fifty years I have seen her only twice. On both occasions we had a nice and civil encounter. By then we were adults with grown children of our own. I came away with a sense of relief that Shamsi, despite her lack of formal education and wild nature, had managed to marry well, create a good life for herself, and establish a business of her own as a beautician. Her feisty nature and good-looks, combined with her street smarts and arrogance, had served her well.

13

Play Iranian Style

Cousin Manooch, now a psychiatrist in the United States, was my childhood buddy—we grew up in Tehran. He was a year younger, I was an inch or two taller, and I loved to boss him around. He had no objection to being bossed around by me, a girl! That created a harmonious relationship between us which resulted in hours of playtime with no fights, bickering, or jealousy—to the delight of our parents.

We were two kids who always found creative ways to entertain ourselves. Our favorite activity was to write scripts for plays and then act them out. Our parents, in turn, were obliged to sit through our theatrical productions; it was the least they could do as a reward for being such good children all day without pestering them.

One hot summer day when our families got together for a day of fun and relaxation, Manooch and I, as usual, resumed our roles as playwrights.

With paper and pencil in hand, we began creating a story for our play. The plot of our drama had to do with a poor, homeless, hungry girl on a cold snowy night with no place to go. I don't remember the details of the plot, but the ending was a happy one: The poor girl is taken in by the father of a well-to-do family to join his children at the dinner table. We must have been aware of class differences in our society, and probably knew something about the behaviors of the rich and the poor. We also knew we were role-playing, so we could pretend to be different characters.

I insisted that Manooch play the part of the poor homeless girl and reserved the role of the benevolent and generous father for myself. He yielded.

To hide my shoulder-length black hair, I made a pony tail and hid it under his school cap, and then put on his long pants. He wore my skirt and blouse, but then his crew cut posed a problem. We could easily fix that. He wore a large white handkerchief on his head and tied a big knot in front, right above his eyebrows. We spent hours cutting white paper, making pretend snowflakes, and rehearsing our lines.

Dinner was over and the grownups adjusted their chairs to face the curtain. We two little geniuses created a stage by tying a rope from one end of the living room wall to the other and hanging my mother's flat sheets over the rope!

Applause, applause, and Manooch entered the stage wearing my clothes. I followed him with a big plastic bucket full of cut paper, pouring snowflakes over his kerchief-covered head. He looked sickly and miserable, moaning and shivering with cold as he said his lines. He coughed and fell down a couple of times. He bent over, as if he was about to throw up—no doubt the effect of cold and snow! He gave the best performance of his life. More applause from the audience! The more snow I poured over his head, the more he shivered and trembled. His parents were proud of their son's natural acting ability. He was a born performer.

The play ended. We changed clothes and came back to the living room. But cousin Manooch's shivering did not stop. My mother stuck a thermometer into his mouth and it registered 102° F—and then he vomited. Manooch missed school for a whole week.

14

The Broken Carousel

When I was five, my favorite place in the whole world was Café Shahrdari, the municipal amusement park. It was a huge park in the center of Tehran. There were puppet shows, marionettes, and an outdoor movie screen. We sat on wooden benches and watched black and white movies of Laurel and Hardy and American westerns. Vendors sold fresh walnuts in funnel-shaped paper bags, grilled corn on the cob dipped in salt water, and saffron-flavored ice cream, sandwiched between two thin wafers. But it was the children's carousel in that park that I loved the most.

The first time Mother took me to ride the carousel I was shaking with excitement. When we approached the far end of the park, where the carousel was located, we saw an angry man foaming at the mouth, cussing, and waving away the children who had come to ride. While holding my hand firmly, my mother suddenly stopped. Then we noticed the little animals on the carousel were all damaged. The angry operator explained to my mother that the little ducks and geese were strictly for little children, but a group of older and heavier teenagers had badly abused the animals, and broken some.

I had looked forward to the ride so much and the disappointment was so great that I began to sob. My mother tried to calm me down, while she sympathized with the carousel operator. She condemned the act, and with the promise to come back another time, gently led me away. I looked back over my shoulder and saw a pale-yellow broken duck with a long neck, orange beak, and sad painted eyes lying flat on the ground. The image stayed with me for a very long time.

Even with the passage of time, I have not abandoned my fascination with riding carousels in amusement parks. When I spot one, no matter where it is, I'm drawn to it like a nail to a magnet. On a trip to California, I saw one in the middle of a busy outdoor shopping mall. A grown woman ardently desiring to ride the carousel must have looked ridiculous and bizarre. But my relatives pretended to be amused by my persistence and a sister-in-law even volunteered to join me on the ride.

Now—with the music floating on the air, horses rising and falling slowly in the breeze—I looked at the canopy above, the platform below, and closed my eyes. It felt heavenly. I imagined myself back in that municipal park halfway around the world, more than half a century ago. If only I could ride a geese or a duck—but all I could find was a jeweled Arabian charger!

15

Tales from the Cellar

Mother loved to take naps after lunch in the *zir zamin*, particularly on hot summer days. I hated taking a nap—it was stupid to waste time sleeping in the middle of the day. But Mother definitely wanted her little snooze after lunch; at the same time she wanted to keep me close by. Often I played with my toys, or drew on papers, or simply let my eyes wander around the cellar.

Once when I was three years old and forced to stay in the *zir zamin,* my mother, in order to keep me occupied, let me play with her gold wedding band! When she was up from her nap, the ring was gone. She inquired and I innocently replied, "I ate the ring!"

She did not believe me at first, but to be on the safe side, I used a chamber pot for a day or two. The content was examined and, sure enough, she found the ring!

Even when I was five, she still forced me to stay in the cellar while she napped. One day it was a hot summer afternoon, and there was nothing to do. I got bored, so I kept looking up through the large lattice window that was the only source of natural light in the *zir zamin.* I kept wondering what was going on in the courtyard above. Of course nothing was going on in that blazing hot summer day.

Suddenly I heard the sound of water, someone was stepping out of the pool. My father, who came home around 2 p.m. for the big midday meal, had gone in for a quick dip.

I moved closer to the window—I could see my father's hairy legs and the end of the towel he had wrapped around his waist. I crept some more and noticed he had stepped onto a low wooden platform which was directly in front of the lattice window. I stretched my neck further and looked straight up. For the first time I saw my father's naked butt, and then his dangling private parts. Instantly I knew it was a sight I was not supposed to see, and quickly withdrew from the window.

As I got older, the cool cellar was the perfect place to stay in during the hot summer days in Tehran, but I never napped there!

16

Book Borrower

Sometime during this period of my life, my father and Uncle Jafar decided to have a bit of remodeling done to the old house. The big *talaar,* which was the scene of many family and neighborhood gatherings, was to be demolished. It had been a place to celebrate happy wedding receptions or sad memorials.

We had to move out while the house renovation was taking place. One block from our house, still on Bouzarjomehri Avenue, a nice-looking house that belonged to a doctor whom my father knew was empty. Temporarily, we moved to this house while the *talaar* was being demolished and re-built.

I don't recall the duration of the construction, but the end results were that the *talaar* was divided into three large rooms. An additional room was put in above the *talaar,* which eventually served as Uncle Jafar's bedroom when he got married.

I was in fourth grade when Uncle Jafar married Mehri, one of the girls from the Badiozamani family. Mother always said it was good to marry into other families and have larger extended relatives. So we did, and added to our relatives since the Badiozamani family had seven children at the time, and eventually ended up with nine.

Aunt Mehri's younger brother, Khosrow, was the one from whom I borrowed my first adventure novel. We didn't have children's or young adult books in the house. So, when Khosrow offered to loan me his book of *Amir Arsalane Namdar,* I gladly accepted. Over seventy years ago, that was the Harry Potter of our time. A handsome hero, Amir Arsalan—tall, strong, dragon-slayer, giant-killer—had many adventures and finally fell in love with a beautiful girl. The book was made into a movie. I still remember the face of the gorgeous-looking girl played by an actress named Roofia. Everyone aahed and oohed as she appeared on the screen because she was the personification of who Amir Arsalan would fall in love with; she looked like the woman we had imagined while reading the book.

I took the book to the cellar with me and read it cover to cover during a summer vacation. But then I forgot about it and tossed it somewhere behind one of the arched nooks in that damp *zir zamin.* A year later, when I finally found the book, it was crumbled, molded, and part of its cover was missing. It was in that condition when I returned the book to my aunt's brother. He looked displeased but didn't say much. Neither did I.

17

The Monitor

We always had a monitor, *mobeser,* in elementary school classes in Tehran, appointed by the teacher. It was prestigious to be a monitor. The mobeser enjoyed certain privileges that other students didn't. A monitor could go into the classroom before the bell rang, while others had to stay outside. She could tidy up the teacher's desk, while others were not allowed to touch anything on the teacher's desk. She could call the roll, snitch on other students, and, in general, be the eyes and ears of the teacher.

Of course, we never knew anything of the selection process and how and why someone got to be our class monitor. I suppose teachers picked students they liked and who they thought had the "management skills" to keep students quiet and in their seats if the teacher was to be late.

In my fifth grade, in a class of 25 girls, our teacher appointed a girl who most of us didn't care for. She was a talkative, arrogant, gum-chewing, self-assured type of a girl. I don't remember her name, but let's call her Gloria. The only thing I knew about her was that her father was a military colonel, and that she had a younger sister in second grade. Since we didn't know her, I think she might have been new to our school.

Her selection as a monitor for our class did not set well with me and my best friend, Soraya. What on earth possessed our teacher to pick Gloria? Maybe it was her lack of shyness and the self-confidence she displayed in talking to teachers. Maybe it was her fearless approach to meeting new people that made our teacher take notice of her.

Thus, Gloria became our class monitor.

The day our teacher was going to be late, we arrived at school to find Gloria already in the classroom. She was wiping the board clean, arranging chalks, touching the big ruler on the teacher's desk, and acting as if she owned the place, or as if she were the real teacher!

Resentment grew in us and we decided we were not going to sit quietly for this arrogant girl. When the bell rang and we entered our class to take our seats, all hell broke loose. Strange sounds and noises were coming from the back of the classroom. Soraya and I always sat in the front row. While Gloria went to the back of the room to put out the "fire" of noises, the rest of us in the first two rows began yakking and creating our own chaos. No one seemed to mind her warnings.

Then Gloria dashed to the front and picked up the long ruler from the teacher's desk. She really wanted to play the role of a teacher, but we were not buying it and resented her all the more.

Soraya and I put our head down on our desk pretending to be crying while in reality we were giggling and making strange noises. Gloria came over with the ruler and gently tapped me on the shoulder. That did it! I sat up and began wailing and—with Soraya as my witness—I declared Gloria had hurt me with the ruler! It was mayhem! It became apparent that none of the other students wanted to have Gloria as our mobeser either. The situation got so out of control that the assistant principal had to intervene and keep us quiet that morning.

Did our teacher regret her choice? I don't know, except that Gloria was no longer our monitor.

The following morning, our teacher held a tribunal in the classroom to find out what really happened the previous day and called upon me to testify!

"Manijeh, you are an impartial, fair-minded student. Explain what happened!" She asked with a smile.

18

Redemption

I'm almost ten years old and in the fourth grade. I walk to and from school with my best friend, Soraya. Our school is tucked in the back of an alley adjacent to the Big Bazaar in downtown Tehran. The school is for girls only. To get there, Soraya and I walk along the Bouzarjomehri Avenue, weave through the street vendors who loudly announce their goods, pass all the shops, go down a set of long, gently-sloped stone stairs, follow a narrow tunnel-like path with bales of cotton piled up high on each side, go through a huge wooden gate, and, voilà, our school is on the right-hand side. This is our shortcut.

The covered bazaar is a thrilling labyrinth branching in many different directions. It is the center of wholesale shopping. Each section offers a particular merchandise: rugs and other floor coverings, spices, gold jewelry, gems, copper and brass products, garments and accessories, china, housewares—you name it. Our shortcut is through the cotton wholesalers' section. Sometimes, as we walk through the narrow walkway, we see a tiny cut in a cotton bale, poke our fingers in, and get out a piece of white fluffy cotton. Soraya and I giggle and take the cotton to school to show other girls. We are used to the crowds and all the noise around us. We pay no attention to the loud sound of hammers banging on the copper plates or the chatter of the workers.

Since we pass through the business section every day, my mother charges me with an important task. I am to give a relatively large sum to a gentleman, the owner of a cosmetics and hosiery store where Mother shops frequently. She puts the money in my school bag with the instructions that, on the way back, I must stop at the store and pay her debt.

During recess, while sitting at my desk next to Soraya, I open my bag. Discreetly I nudge at her elbow to call her attention to my open school bag. With our heads touching, we both hover over my bag to look at the large bill. The fact that I'm entrusted with such a large sum is a matter of pride. It makes me feel grownup and reliable.

After school, we both walk together and make a stop at the designated store. Proud that I'm doing an errand for my mother, I open my bag. But the money isn't there! The bill has vanished. Soraya and I search high and low. The store owner looks at us with a smile but doesn't say anything. I empty the entire content of my bag on the counter—no money.

Feelings of fright, embarrassment, bewilderment, and sadness put my stomach in a knot. Whatever happened to the money? I can't figure it out—it was there a few hours ago. We walk home in utter silence. Soraya is pensive and I'm frightened. How am I to face my mother? All I can think of is my own failure to complete one task she asked me to do. I'm so disappointed in myself.

My lips quiver, and I try to hold back the tears as I tell my mother I lost the bill. Her first reaction is a quick whack on the side of my head. She looks at me indignantly and asks,

"How could you do that?"

I cannot hold back the tears any longer. The knot in my stomach moves up to my throat and releases itself through tears. I cry not because she hits me, but because I feel terribly stupid, incapable of carrying out a task. But she calms down quickly when my father whispers something in her ears. The matter is dropped and never mentioned again.

Two years pass, and I am about to graduate from elementary school. My parents have bought a house in a different part of town and we are moving out of the Big Bazaar neighborhood. On the last day of school, all the girls hug and wish each other well in the upcoming seventh grade. Soraya and I will be going to different secondary schools on opposite sides of Tehran.

Suddenly a girl who has been in my class all along approaches me. She is a plain-looking quiet sort who has never been in our circle of friends. Actually I don't recall if she has ever talked to me.

I smile at her, but she doesn't look at me. With downcast eyes and trembling voice she says she is the one who took the money out of my school bag two years ago, "I'm asking for forgiveness."

I look at her with mouth agape and wide eyes. Why is she confessing after all this time? I really have nothing to say. I have forgotten the incident.

She continues, "My mother forced me to come and tell you, so the money would not be *haram*" (unlawful).

She hastily adds that at the time her father was out of work and the family needed the money.

A tingling starts in my stomach, finds its way all the way up to my face, and I flash a broad, friendly smile at the girl. It had never ever occurred to me that someone might have taken the money. I can hardly wait to report to my mother that I was not careless; I was robbed.

As gently as a twelve-year-old can be, I assure her that she has nothing to worry about. The money is *halal* (lawful).

She is forgiven.

19

Ramadan and Fastings

The long-sleeved dress hides the black and blue marks on my upper arms. We are visiting Aunt Tooran at the Misaghieh Hospital. She has given birth to a little girl. Mother and I walk into the maternity ward. Aunt Tooran is in bed—she looks good. She is older than my mother by three years, but she married later and this is her first child.

Mother sits on a chair by the side of the bed and the two sisters start talking in hushed quiet voices. I stay standing near my mother. Mom recounts the events of the previous day, and then grabs one of my arms, pulls up the sleeve to show her sister the black and blue marks on my skinny arm inflicted by my father's angry hands the day before. I'm totally embarrassed.

It is the month of Ramadan in the Muslim world—a full month of fasting. In our household, the only folks who fast are Aziz, my father's aunt, and Homa, her teenage daughter. Those two are the devout souls who fast the entire month. No one else in my house fasts. Dad and Uncle Jafar talk of their duodenal ulcers and say they cannot go without food for the whole day. Mother's fasting is sporadic; it depends on whether or not she needs to shed a few pounds.

What intrigues me about Ramadan is the ritual that Aziz and Homa follow during the entire month. They get up before the sunrise to prepare for the morning meal, *sahari.* They start the samovar to boil water for tea. They warm up the left-over meal from the night before, whatever it may be: rice, lamb stew with herbs, or cutlets. I love the staples at the *sahari:* bread sprinkled with sesame seeds, a dish of walnut and raisins, and a chunk of feta cheese on the side. I'm eager to get up early and be part of this ritual.

Also, I'm enchanted by the singing of the muezzin whose voice I hear through a loudspeaker from the nearby mosque located in the Big Bazaar. The loudspeaker rotates, and I hear the voice of the muezzin sometimes close by, sometimes from afar. He sings the prayers from the Quran, and in the quiet early morning hours it sounds like an angel's voice from heaven.

I'm eleven years old and a skinny girl. My parents constantly give me vitamins and cod liver oil so that I may gain weight and get stronger. I hate cod liver oil. The sight of the bottle with its yellowish color and the fishy smell makes me throw up. I'm in the habit of closing my eyes, pinching my nose between my thumb and index finger, and opening my mouth so that Mother can shove a spoonful of the oil into my mouth. They believe it will make me stronger and gain weight—everyone thinks being thin is undesirable.

It is fine with my parents if I'm only an observer of Aziz and Homa's ritual during Ramadan. The problem begins when a few of my classmates, including my best friend Soraya, come to school and announce they are fasting. I want to fast, too!

Aziz knows how my parents feel about this business of fasting. She makes sure to perform her morning ritual quietly so I don't wake up early in the morning. But my desire to fast just like my friends makes me wake myself up and join Aziz and Homa. They have already finished their morning meal. Despite Aziz's objection, I quickly drink a cup of tea and swallow a piece of bread and later declare to my parents that I'm fasting and refuse to eat breakfast.

At midday I refuse to eat lunch too. A first, my parents show patience. They try to reason with me to break my fast, but I don't eat. My stubbornness exacerbates my father and puts him into a rage. He is so angry that he grabs me by both my arms, and in the heat of his anger sinks his fingers into my skinny arms and gives me a good shake. I break my fast and eat.

Years pass by. I get older and stronger, and read research articles about the actual health benefits of fasting that go beyond the religious implications: cleansing of the body and mind, abstaining from harmful habits such as smoking, experiencing hunger in order to have compassion for the poor and the hungry. But I never fast again! For me, Ramadan and fasting remain memories laced with fear, anger, sadness, and embarrassment.

20

Bitter Memory of a Summer Camp

After my freshman year in high school, my parents agreed to send me to a summer camp by the Caspian Sea. Oh, how much I looked forward to this adventure! I'd heard stories about the exciting activities and fun times girls had enjoyed at these camps. It wasn't just the fun, but also the prestige that was attached to attending. Not everyone was selected to attend. There were age limits and required recommendations, not to mention (perhaps) some connections here and there, which helped with the selection process.

Having completed my freshman year of high school, I was old enough to participate, but maybe a bit on the younger side. With a little help from Uncle Jafar, who knew the camp director, I was accepted to spend ten days at the seaside; an adventure organized and, I assume, funded by the Ministry of Education. It was going to be a new experience for me: away from home, fun activities, camp fires, swimming, and a lot of laughter with high school girls my age.

On that memorable day of departure, my parents took me to where I was supposed to board the bus, along with other participants, heading north to the Caspian seaside. There must have been over 150 girls in that parking area, from various high schools in Tehran. Eight buses were ready to take bubbly, chattering teen girls and their suitcases to Ramsar for a camping and vacation adventure.

I boarded the last bus—bus number eight—and sat in the third row behind the bus driver. Next to me sat a sweet girl about two years older than I was, a new friend. She was a senior from a different high school. I had met her a week earlier when my mother and I were clothes shopping for the camping trip.

We chatted as the bus started: our schools, classes, and the fun we were going to have at the camp. It was her first time traveling north to the Caspian. We left the outskirts of Tehran and took the winding, mountainous road of Chaloos toward Ramsar. Being the last bus, obviously we trailed the others.

Somewhere along the way, being last did not agree with our driver and he took it upon himself to speed up and pass another bus on that narrow mountainous road. The first time he did it the kids on the bus clapped and cheered him on.

Of the two teachers who were supposed to be our chaperones on that bus, one was sitting in the first row right behind the driver, and the other one, a gentleman, was at the back of the bus playing cards with some students. They never raised any objections to the speed or the driver's behavior.

On our first rest stop, however, I noticed the lady chaperone switched buses and didn't board ours! The driver, a short hefty man with a shaved head, decided to repeat his stunt: speed up and pass the next bus. Near Siabisheh, a small rural town where the road narrowed, with high mountains on one side and a deep ravine on the other, is where it all happened.

I was sitting near the window on the ravine side, and periodically looked down and saw a shallow river way down flowing at the bottom of the ravine. Suddenly our driver lost control of the speeding bus; he swerved, hit the side of the mountain, and then swerved again and plunged down into the deep ravine. All I remember was a peculiar sensation and a sight like watching a fast-moving slide show—of us slamming into the mountain side, with bushes and trees passing by with the speed of light. I gently closed my eyes and lost consciousness.

As if waking up from a deep sleep, with half-opened eyes, I saw blurred silhouettes hovering over me, grabbing my arms trying to pull me out. I didn't know it at the time, but the bus had rolled and landed upside down at the bottom of the ravine with water, rocks, pebbles, and small boulders with sharp edges. How long it had been, how I was thrown out of the bus, or how I was now under the bus, I have no recollection. All I felt was the excruciating pain caused by the sharp edges of the rocks that were piercing my back.

I moaned, weakly, and a man's voice said, "Slow, slow, don't pull her out too fast; clear the rocks first."

He was part of a group of local peasants who had seen the accident and had rushed down to the scene, with their spades, to help the victims.

How I got to the small local hospital, I don't remember. My next recollection is sitting in a hospital room with nothing in it except a bed. Next to me sat my newfound friend. She and I had no visible or dramatic physical injuries, no obvious bleeding—nothing that according to the local medical staff needed immediate and fast attention. We both sat in that room, in a daze, shivering and hungry as it was late in the afternoon and we had not eaten anything since we had left home early that morning.

After an hour, a young man—whether a curious local resident or a hospital staff, I didn't know which—poked his head in to see who was in the room. My friend said we were terribly hungry. He smiled and walked away but came back within a few minutes with some bread and cheese for us to munch on. We then ventured to walk out of our room to see what was going on in that small local hospital.

"Oh God, we must have been among your chosen people," I thought.

What I saw in the hallway and other rooms came back as nightmares on many occasions later: broken and bleeding noses, broken legs and arms, head injuries, and lacerations. A little later I learned a girl had lost her life in the accident—she had been sitting in a row directly in front of me.

We went back to the room and sat there waiting for some camp official to come and get us. Nothing happened until 9 p.m. Then I heard noises. Two ladies walked into the room. One was a colleague of my uncle's who was in charge of the summer camp—probably appointed by the Minister of Education. The other lady must have been her deputy. In an official car driven by a chauffeur, they must have left Tehran to come and inspect the scope of the injuries.

Curiously enough, they exchanged words and comments in English! I knew some English so I could understand and pick up their extreme sense of fright and concern. They were planning to head on directly to the camp after the hospital visit.

They were about to leave our room, relieved that at least these two girls had no obvious injuries, when a voice inside my head said,

"You don't want to be left alone in this hospital by yourself. Say something."

Immediately I blurted out my name, with the emphasis on my last name. Uncle Jafar was well-known among the educators, athletes, and the Ministry of Education officials. Upon hearing the name, the ladies exchanged glances, and one of them quickly said,

"Why don't you two girls get into the car and come with us to the camp."

I climbed into the back seat wearing a torn and blood-stained dress, and my friend sat next to me. The two ladies continued their dialogue in English. Unbeknownst to them I basically understood whatever they said. Their major concerns were the newspaper headlines the next day, the reaction of the ministry officials, and who was going to be found responsible for this accident, particularly now that a young student had died.

It was almost midnight when we arrived at the camp. The news of the bus accident had reached the camp—other buses had arrived safely and the girls were in their respective tents. I was put in a tent with two other girls, sleeping on a cot.

When a bugle sounded the wakeup call in the morning, I opened my eyes. I was alive and I was at the camp. As soon as I attempted to raise my head and sit up, my entire body reacted violently with such excruciating pain that I almost stopped breathing. I had no choice but to lie still and not to move a muscle. Every little movement of my body parts inflicted a horrific pain. The shock of the accident, the inverted bus, the sharp rocks and boulders on my back all played a part.

Breakfast was not even over at the camp when I saw my parents and Uncle Jafar walk into the tent. It is difficult for a fifteen-year-old to understand the scope and depth of anxiety and anguish parents feel in such a situation: to send their child to a camp in the morning and hear the bus crashed in the afternoon. My parents had to see with their own eyes that I was alive. They had come to take me back home. But, of course, I didn't want to leave! I had looked forward to this camp for so long. Obviously I was not in any shape, physically or emotionally, to participate in any of the activities.

That morning my parents took me to a medical clinic in Ramsar and had me X-rayed from head to toe for internal injuries. They ignored my stubbornness on insisting to stay at the camp! Once they were sure I had no internal injuries, we had a nice afternoon tea and pastries at the nearby Hotel Ramsar. It was my newfound friend who convinced me it was in my best interest to forget about the camp and go back home with my parents.

And good advice it was! A day later I came down with a severe case of influenza that landed me in bed for two weeks. However, it took me almost a year to get over the trauma of the accident and the phobia of riding in a car or a bus. I never applied for the summer camp again.

21

Passing on a Tradition

The summer before my junior year in high school, my family rented a vacation place in the village of Meygoon, tucked in the mountains, roughly a two-hour drive northeast of Tehran. We were to share this place with the Davar family—Mrs. Davar was my father's second cousin. This summer place was on a fifteen-acre walled piece of property, part of which had been turned into an orchard. The house itself consisted of only two very large, plain, empty rooms made of bricks and cement. A raised veranda extended in front of both rooms. There was no kitchen. The only outhouse, with a wooden door, was located in a corner on the west end of the property. A narrow stream ran through the orchard and our drinking water was hauled in every day from a nearby well. There was nothing else. Bare essentials for the duration of our stay were brought in from the city.

I don't know what prompted my parents to rent this place. Maybe they were plotting to test how their children fared in a camp-like condition for two months. It was a test of endurance and survival disguised as getting away from the scorching heat of summer in Tehran.

Maybe my father's intent was not only to get away from the heat, but also to teach us a lesson and make us appreciate the comfort of our home. But we were oblivious to all the shortcomings of the place and the subtle lessons we were supposed to learn.

Mr. Davar and my father hiked, played backgammon, and discussed the possibility of buying this piece of property together. They spent hours inspecting the orchard and counting the trees. They were taking inventory just in case they decided to purchase the place.

Our main source of entertainment was the steady stream of visitors who showed up without prior notice. Relatives and friends who had been invited to drop in accepted the invitation without hesitation. They usually stayed for a night or two, escaping the heat of the city. They brought plenty of food, their musical instruments (if they played any), and sleeping bags, and camped out on the property. They also brought their children, all younger than I.

One weekend, our neighbor in Tehran showed up with her two daughters. Sheila, the older one, was nearly twelve years old. She was an extremely attractive girl, a bit on the chubby side, with long black hair and gorgeous eyes and long dark lashes.

On one memorable afternoon, when all the grown-ups were taking naps after a heavy midday meal and the younger children were scattered around the orchard, I was stretched on a rug at the far end of the veranda reading a novel. Suddenly, several children came running and with a mixture of anxiety and excitement announced there was trouble at the outhouse. They reported Sheila had locked herself inside and was not coming out unless I went there to talk to her.

Reluctantly, but with a tinge of curiosity, I put down my book and walked towards the outhouse, followed by half a dozen little boys and girls of various ages. Chattering constantly, they complained about not being able to use the outhouse because of Sheila.

I knocked on the wooden door and called her name. Upon hearing my voice, Sheila unlocked the door and let me in. Standing in a corner of that semi-lit place, she was trembling and looked pale as a ghost. I could see panic in her big brown eyes. She was holding her underpants in her hand. Without a word, she stretched her arms and showed me her underwear with blood stains.

I chuckle every time I think of what happened next. Just like my aunt, who had slapped me on the face several years earlier when I started my period, I smiled from ear to ear, and slapped Sheila on the face, on both cheeks! If I had not smiled, I'm sure the poor girl would have fainted thinking she was being punished for some unknown sin she had committed. However, with an aura of authority and confidence, and still smiling, I explained to her, just the way it was explained to me, that slapping her face would bring her good luck and that it would also preserve her rosy cheeks. What on earth slapping had to do with menstruation and a rosy complexion, I didn't know. I was merely passing on a tradition.

I assured Sheila she was not sick and had done nothing wrong. By this time, the children were banging on the door, demanding an explanation. A few were threatening to pee in their pants. Quickly, we had to come up with a story. I opened the door and calmly announced there was a bullfrog in the outhouse and it had frightened Sheila. It was the only excuse I could think of at that particular moment. Immediately, I regretted my choice when all the children screamed with excitement and rushed in to see the bullfrog.

22

Banu Khanoom

The legend of Banu Khanoom always preceded her. Many parents sent their daughters to the prestigious Anoushiravan Dadgar High School because of her. This private, all female secondary school had earned the reputation of being one of the best in the city of Tehran, and Banu Khanoom was a permanent fixture in that school. She was the assistant principal in charge of attendance and discipline.

When I started seventh grade in that school, Banu Khanoom looked old already. But she probably was in her early forties. She was barely five feet tall and on the heavy side; I could never decide if she was round or square! Her silvery white hair was parted in the middle and always pulled back and gathered into a bun slightly above her short neck.

She must have had a limited wardrobe because she always wore the same simple gray suit—a jacket that covered her big hips and a straight skirt. Needless to say, one could never trace a speck of makeup on her face. The combination of her hairstyle, clothing, and stern and plain face scared the daylight out of students. We all feared and respected her.

The school had been established by a group of Zoroastrians, the original Parsi religion. Banu Khanoom was a Zoroastrian herself. She was strict in the true sense of the word. I never saw her smile or laugh during all the years I attended that school. As if being in charge of discipline meant having a serious face with a perpetual frown! Her trademark was a long wooden ruler that she held firmly with both hands behind her as she walked through the halls.

I was in my sophomore year when the movie Helen of Troy found its way to Tehran. The ponytail hairstyle became fashionable among teenagers. Those with long hair pulled their hair way up and held it with a rubber band. I followed suit.

One day I was walking down the long hall towards my class when suddenly I heard a voice behind me. I froze in place and my heart fell to my knees. I recognized her voice, "Why you, Golbabai, of all the people? I cannot believe it!"

I turned around, and faced Banu Khanoom. I trembled inside, but managed a faint smile and tried to greet her. She continued, "I absolutely did not expect it from you! After all you are from a good family."

Not knowing what she was talking about, I ventured, "But Banu Khanoom, what have I done wrong?"

I was about to cry. If she didn't kill me right then, the suspense of not knowing what on earth I had done would kill me! She pointed to my ponytail and with clenched teeth asked, "What is this? You should be braiding your hair."

Right then and there, she made me take the elastic band off and let my long hair down. To her, it was a disgrace to wear one's hair in a ponytail, like the Helen of Troy actress. She thought a girl from a nice family should not wear a ponytail. Banu Khanoom had her own standards of morality, model behavior, and purity.

The girls at Anoushiravan Dadgar High School were not the only ones who were scared of Banu Khanoon. Her reputation had reached beyond our walled campus to the nearby private all male secondary school, Alborz High School, where Uncle Jafar had been an assistant principal for many years. It was only a block north of my school.

In order not to let the students of these two high schools have any contact with each other at the end of the school day, we were dismissed a half hour earlier than our male counterparts. Banu Khanoom wanted to make sure all "her girls" were safely out of the street, before the male beasts were let out of their cage. For this reason, she normally walked from the gate of our school campus to the main street and stood watch, still holding her big stick. God forbid if a young man lingered or even attempted to approach and say "hello" to a uniform-clad girl from Anoushiravan Dadgar High School. Banu Khanoom was the defender of the honor and chastity of all of us.

And then I came to the United States during my senior year to attend an American high school—well that is the subject of a totally different book!

23

High School Prank

We are juniors at the prestigious all female Anoushiravan Dadgar High School in Tehran. As upper classmates, we are considered mature and enjoy a relaxed relationship with our teachers and the administrators.

The assistant principal in charge of attendance and discipline for the junior and senior classes is a middle-aged woman whose personality is the total opposite of Banu Khanoom, the assistant principal in charge of discipline for the lower classes, who had made us tremble in our boots when we heard her voice! Yes, Banu Khanoom with her usual stern face and thin tight lips is still firmly planted in her office on the first floor, but we have already been molded into models of good behavior. It is the younger students who need to be whipped into shape. Our new assistant principal is friendly and lenient towards us. We all like her because she smiles often and maintains a good rapport with the senior and junior students.

A relative of my mother returns from the United States and brings back some interesting items as gifts. He has bought them at hobby shops around Halloween—though at the time I know nothing about Halloween. These items are goofy large eyeballs, funny glasses with an attached plastic nose, and whoopee cushions. One item particularly interests me: a glob of brown plastic which realistically resembles human excrement. I ask if I can have the item—he smiles and graciously hands it over!

The next day, I hide the plastic glob in the pocket of my uniform and head for school. Arriving very early, I walk into our classroom, put the plastic excrement on the teacher's chair, and walk away swiftly, closing the door behind me. We, the students, stay in a fixed classroom while the teachers rotate.

Students begin to arrive on the second floor. We usually stand around, talk, and wait for the bell to ring before entering the classroom. The bell rings, and I make sure I'm the first one entering the class.

Casually, I pass by the teacher's desk, let out a loud cry, and hold my nose between my thumb and the index finger. Gasping for air, I point to the fake human feces on the teacher's chair. All hell breaks loose. Girls are screaming and running out of the class, yelling for the janitor to come and open the windows. A few girls run to the office of the new assistant principal to notify her of the "huge mess" in our class. Some with overactive imaginations also report having seen a puddle of "pee" around the feces.

The janitor, an old man with drooping shoulders, slowly opens the door to our classroom, while thirty of us gather in the hall right behind him. Holding a small broom in one hand and a bucket in the other, the old man cautiously kicks the door open, as if there is a beast in there waiting to jump out. As soon as the old man steps one foot into the classroom, he withdraws his body immediately and promptly faints. It is only for a few seconds, because he gasps for air and says the odor has overwhelmed him.

Imaginations are running wild, and the speculation on "who done it" is flying around. The names of a few unpopular girls in the lower grades are mentioned as possible suspects. The commotion is getting out of control. With the help of some girls, the janitor is slowly getting up on his feet.

From the corner of my eye, I catch a glimpse of the new assistant principal getting out of her office, which is located down the hall on the same floor. She is heading towards us.

Amidst all the confusion, I slip into the classroom, grab the plastic glob, put it back into my pocket, and slip away. A few girls are walking and chatting with the assistant principal, informing her of all the details, and the story grows larger by the seconds.

She and the janitor walk together into the classroom. The brown glob is gone and the teacher's chair is clean. By this time it is mass hysteria! Some firmly believe the unpopular student who had committed this despicable act has seized the moment and cleaned up her mess.

I can no longer wait and truly do not want anybody to get into trouble. I walk over to the assistant principal and extend my right arm with the fake brown feces smack in the middle of my palm. There is a moment of absolute silence. She gazes at it for a few seconds and then slowly touches it with the tip of her index finger—still not believing it is actually made of plastic! Finally, she takes it out of my hand. All the girls are watching her face intently for a clue as to how to react.

With her spectacles on the tip of her nose, she peers over this fake realistic replica of human excrement. A moment of silence that seems like an eternity to me is broken by her exclamation:

"Holy …..! This is incredible!" and then she lets out a loud laugh.

I don't get into trouble, but she does ask me if she can borrow the glob for a couple of days!

Part II

Relatives and
Other Stories

24

Two Brothers

As a child, I was fortunate to have the love of two men. I grew up feeling as if I had two very caring fathers: Hassan and Jafar. I have never seen two brothers so close, so devoted to each other's families, and with such deep love and respect for each other.

My father's caring for Jafar sometimes extended beyond brotherly love. At times, it appeared as if Uncle Jafar were my father's son, although Dad was only two years older. Their unique relationship stemmed from the fact that they had lost their father when they were young and had become extremely protective of one another.

Amazingly, despite their closeness and similar background and experiences, they were also different in many respects, such as their reactions to life and approaches to parenting. The differences sometimes were like day and night.

My father worked for the government and travelled all over Iran for extended periods. During his long absences, Uncle Jafar became the father figure. They both had served in the army and then left the military to pursue civilian work. My father took a government job, and Uncle Jafar became a teacher. Their similar experiences, however, did not translate into similar reactions to daily life situations.

Without doubt my father was an authoritative figure. No one questioned his wisdom and sincerity because he truly cared for his family and the people around him. However, his words were the absolute "rule of law," and deviation from those rules had consequences.

We were a comfortable family, yet he was most frugal when it came to spending for what he considered frivolous items, such as fancy clothes or extra pairs of shoes. Material things were not of importance to him. What he valued the most was education. He never refused to spend money on education and what he considered "expanding one's mind." I didn't have as many pretty clothes like some of my friends (my mother made all my clothes), but he would spend money to hire expensive tutors so I could learn a foreign language or excel in math.

My father read constantly in every discipline: psychology, philosophy, history, literature, and religion. I still remember his exact words: "Material things can be taken away overnight, but what you store in your brain stays with you no matter where you go in the world; no one can take away your knowledge."

My father had a quick temper—God forbid if I did not obey his instructions! I never doubted his affection for me, but his fiery temper was something I tried to avoid at all costs. It was futile to disagree with my father. He was the authority and the commander-in-chief.

In contrast, Uncle Jafar had a calm demeanor combined with a tremendous sense of humor. He rarely got angry. If I were unruly or uncooperative as a child—which I sometimes was—he would show his displeasure in my behavior by frowning or raising his eyebrows.

Uncle Jafar was not a book worm, but magazines, newspapers, and current events were his passion. He read the daily papers cover to cover and he was well-informed of what was happening in our city. He loved movies and never missed a single new film in town.

He was an assistant principal at Alborz, a prestigious private all-male high school. He gained the reputation for being a well-respected film critic. His students always consulted him regarding new movies and respected his opinion on what was actually worth watching.

Unlike my father, who was not interested in sports, Uncle Jafar was very much into athletics. His college degree was in physical education. When I was five years old, he took me to see a boxing match. He introduced me to basketball by taking me to see the Harlem Globe Trotters when they came to Tehran. He refereed fencing matches and often took me along to watch—I was nine years old at the time.

It was Uncle Jafar who arranged for me and my sister to take swimming lessons at an athletic club, where we spent many hot summer days. Uncle Jafar was also generous with his money and often gave me presents. It was relaxing to be around Uncle Jafar. He injected humor into our daily lives.

I loved both these men equally; it was like having two fathers. I'm the lucky beneficiary of their differences in parenting style.

25

My Mother's Aunt

More than half a century ago, in a male-dominated society in the Middle East, lived a courageous woman. She had no education, worked at different jobs, and raised two very decent children all by herself. This amazing woman, who challenged society, defied its archaic rules, and treasured her own financial independence up to the end was my mother's aunt.

Because of her lack of formal schooling, she could hardly read or write, but she had the courage and the iron will to get jobs in order to support her family, a rare occurrence over 70 years ago in a society where women were treated like second-class citizens. She was a lion-hearted woman. When I try to visualize her, for some very strange reason I think of her as the female version of John Wayne. Maybe it was her physical features that remind me of the actor. She was tall and muscular. Her eyes were small and penetrating. Most definitely it was the shape of her mouth and thin lips that resembled John Wayne.

She was not particularly attractive. Her grayish hair, reaching her shoulders, was usually pulled back with a rubber band, or sometimes shaped into a bun. I don't ever recall seeing her wearing make-up or lipstick. She was plain-looking with a full round face. Smack in the middle of her face was a big nose. A round pinkish colored wart was nestled on the left side of her nose that was hard to ignore. She had a quick tongue, with a temper to match. Her husband had divorced her when her two children, a boy and a girl, were toddlers.

My early memories of my mother's aunt go back to the time when she rented the small house adjacent to ours, and she became our next-door neighbor. By then, her daughter was attending a boarding school and was training to become a nurse. Her son was already grown and had a job.

Even with no education at all, she held a series of jobs—from being a nanny at the home of a well-known government official, to managing the laundry section of a boarding school for a teacher-training college. She also served, as she put it, as the "keeper of the keys" for the science labs in one of the prestigious high schools in her hometown. I'm sure she was given other duties besides being the keeper of the laboratory keys! Although she had no formal education, her innate smarts and her sheer determination to be independent had landed her different jobs and had made her a favorite person at whatever institution she worked. The government official, whose children were raised by her, had secured her a permanent government job, making sure Dear Auntie drew regular paychecks. So she was officially hired by the department of education and retired after thirty years of service.

Dear Auntie, or *Khaleh Joon,* as we affectionately called her, was also known as "Queen of Clean." Her dwellings were absolutely immaculate. Because she was so impeccably clean and tidy, her visits to our house made my mother feel a bit anxious. Mother made sure the contents of the cabinets were organized and that the house was cleaned up before her aunt arrived.

Regardless of Mother's agonizing moments of getting everything into shape prior to her aunt's visit, when *Khaleh Joon* arrived, she invariably re-organized the closets and the cabinets. Everything in my mother's closets would be taken out. *Khaleh Joon* would then sit on the Persian rug and meticulously inspect and organize every article of clothing. She would neatly fold the contents of Mother's underwear drawers and then move on to her party clothes and evening wear. This activity not only kept *Khaleh Joon* busy, but also gave her a chance to find out what new clothing items my mother had acquired. *Khaleh Joon* was very curious and nosy about this sort of thing. But she was good at organizing and re-arranging, and usually by the time she was done with her self-imposed task, I could see a smile of gratitude on my mother's face.

Upon her retirement, *Khaleh Joon* was available and willing to help out family members for various occasions, such as weddings, huge dinner parties, or the birth of a child. *Khaleh Joon's* expertise, patience, and know-how always came in handy. When my youngest sister, Zoe, was born she came and stayed at our house for a few weeks to help run the household.

Khaleh Joon was also a fabulous cook and passed her skills on to her own daughter. On the occasions when she invited us to her tiny place for dinner, we knew we were in for a treat. She always had an assortment of stews: eggplant with lamb, *Khoresht Bademjan;* herb stew, *Ghormeh Sabzi;* or meatballs in pomegranate and walnut sauce, *Khoresht Fesenjan;* all served over steaming saffron rice. Homemade chutney and jams were her specialties, which she served with flat bread. For dessert, she had various melons in season, along with traditional candies and cookies.

Khaleh Joon zealously guarded and preserved her own financial independence. This was truly something to behold, given the era and the country in which she lived. She was not schooled, but she had learned a lot in the college of life. She was organized and managed her household budget well on whatever she made. She invited relatives for meals, gave gifts to the children for *Norouz,* and, as I learned later, she had even purchased a cemetery plot and put aside funds for her own funeral service years in advance.

One story told by my mother sums up *Khaleh Joon's* strong and fearless character. One night a burglar came to her house. Dear Auntie's sharp hearing alerted her to the presence of an intruder. She immediately set out to catch the burglar. The man tried to flee, but somehow this lion-hearted lady managed to grab the burglar by his testicles, and with her strong, mighty hands she had held on and squeezed till the neighbors and the police arrived.

She was illiterate, but not ignorant. She had no formal schooling but was far more intelligent than some who were schooled. *Khaleh Joon* had wisdom, common sense, and had experienced life. She was a unique lady and a feminist in her own way more than half a century ago.

Ironically, only recently did I learn of her actual last name, "Hamedanchi Azad." Apparently, everyone called her "Mrs. Azad." The word *Azad* in Persian language means "free." A befitting name for a woman who was truly free up to the end!

26

Portrait of an Iranian Marriage

Her white wedding gown, the tiara, her heavily made-up face, and the profile of the groom sitting next to her all were reflected in the big mirror in front of her. Jubilant family members danced around to the beat of the drum and the jingle of the tambourine, and clapped their hands. Her mother wept quietly with joy; after all she had raised her singlehandedly, without a husband, all by herself.

She looked like any other bride: a bit shy, downcast eyes, and docile-looking. She didn't smile much—one had to be ladylike. She had always been on the plump side. With her small blue eyes, fair skin, and curly light-brown hair she looked a bit different than the other Iranian girls her age. She was still in school hoping to become a nurse's aide, or a nurse, eventually. But when the agents for a suitor showed up knocking on her door, she opted for marriage.

The agents who came for a visit were the sister and aunt of the future groom. They came to check her out and learn about her family. As tradition required, they reported back their findings to the young man. Several visits later, she met the man who was to be her husband.

No sparks were generated in the young man's heart when they met. He was rather aloof and lukewarm towards her. But the sister and the aunt persisted, and he eventually yielded and the two became engaged. The groom's mother had passed away and the aunt, in essence, considered herself a second mother. The groom's sister, good-looking and rather large in body, was not married. She decided this particular young lady would make a suitable wife and companion for her brother and a good sister-in-law to her. The aunt's position was ambivalent. They were not far off in their assessment, for the future bride was indeed an accomplished homemaker—she had learned from the best, her own mother.

The wedding ceremony and reception took place at the spacious house and garden of a relative. The groom's face was void of emotion or excitement. For him, it was a loveless union of convenience—marrying a nice girl whom his sister approved of. But the bride was smitten right away by this young man's good looks and charming personality—so were others who came in contact with him. He was friendly, sociable, and absolutely devoted to his own side of the family: an old widower father; three brothers, all single; an unmarried sister; and, of course, the dear old auntie who behaved as if she were the mother of the family.

The young bride was an ideal woman with regards to the affairs of the kitchen, an excellent cook, and a perfect hostess. Her dinner parties were flawless and the talk of the family. No doubt she tried desperately to enter her husband's heart through his stomach. Did it work? Maybe for a little while, because they ended up with three children!

Immediately after the birth of her first child, a daughter, a harsh and bitter argument ensued between her and the belligerent aunt. They did not get along—it was a power struggle between the two women. Unfortunately, her husband always took sides with his dear auntie. This internal family feud and power struggle were never-ending, with jabbing words and remarks flying in the air. Such a constant struggle, which would have worn out any ordinary woman, strengthened her resolve and made her more determined to hang on to her husband, despite his cold shoulder and indifference toward her.

The next two children, both boys, arrived a few years later, but her husband's aloof behavior and deliberate coldness didn't alter. For him, it was a convenient married life. He had a wife who adored him, three beautiful children, and his business was taking off and booming. What else was there for him to do but to find excitement and sexual satisfaction with women other than his wife?

She slowly learned of his indiscretions and infidelities. But in a culture where freedom is allowed to the male of the species to do as they please—as long as they take care of the family financially—she seemingly had nothing to complain about. Indeed, he was a good provider. She never lacked for money, but true love and emotional attachment were missing from her life. He simply didn't care and ignored her emotional needs. What can one do with one-sided love?

Her children grew up, and he became a well-known business leader. He provided financial security for his family, but still refused to give her the one thing she yearned for: genuine love and affection. This was an ever-present ugly and unspoken truth in her life.

The boys moved to America, and because of their father's generous investments they could open their own businesses and enjoy comfortable lives. When she came to visit her sons, she stayed and never went back. Thus began a separation of more than two decades, with oceans between them, until she passed away.

Her sons did their utmost to compensate for their father's lack of affection toward their mother and showered her with unconditional love. But the unanswered question always loomed in the air: did her son's devotion ever compensate for the absence of love from her husband.

27

An Iranian Stepmother

He was barely two years old when his beautiful mother died of stomach cancer. His father grieved long and hard for the loss of his young wife. He did not remarry for several years, despite his family's insistence that he should take a wife at least for the sake of the young child.

The child was six when the father remarried. Smitten by the look of a young woman he had seen in the street, he sent his relatives to inquire about the young woman's family and report back to him—that was the social custom at the time. Families got involved, and expressed opinions.

The report on the young woman and her family was sketchy: her family was unrefined, the young woman was plump but pleasant-looking, she was arrogant with not much education or social grace. They warned him, but the man persisted. They got married, and now the young boy had a stepmother.

Jealousy is a complex emotion, and always involves a third party seen as a rival for affection. Who was the rival for the affection of the father? The tiny six-year-old boy, or the image of a beautiful young first wife who had died in the prime of her life? No one could have imagined the extent of jealousy and animosity the stepmother showed towards the little boy. Her cruelty took the form of insane and psychotic physical punishments such as burning the kid's skin with a cigarette, banging the kid's head on the wall, hitting, and God knows what else!

Obviously, the meek husband demonstrated no moral strength to stand up to his wife's cruel behavior. Thus, he would turn to the elders in the family to help him. In a culture where the words and advice of elders are respected and accepted, this woman openly defied and ridiculed everyone, and continued on her own path of viciousness. Cultural taboos of the time prevented reporting such events to law enforcement agencies. These matters were usually handled within families, with intervention from the elders.

The saga continued and the stepmother became pregnant and gave birth to a little girl. One would think becoming a mother herself would soften her heart to show kindness and compassion to the stepson. But that was hardly the case. At times, relatives wondered whether the husband ever regretted his own decision!

Years went by and somehow the elders gave up on giving advice or intervening in his marriage. The couple ended up having three children together and, through it all, the wife was the matriarch of the family.

No matter how difficult life is, children eventually grow up. The physical scars inflicted by his stepmother's brutality healed. But did he ever get rid of the emotional scars? Was he able to get over his psychological trauma? Everyone wondered.

In his adult life, he became a quiet, soft-spoken, and caring individual. He ended up with a family of his own: a loving wife and three children. Sadly, he passed away after a long illness.

28

Uncle Razmi

Of all the characters I encountered while growing up, none was more colorful and fascinating to me than Razmi.

Razmi was a retired army colonel, and quarter of a century older than my father. We all called him Uncle Razmi. If I want to think of a family secret, or a puzzling question to answer in this book, probably Razmi's relation to my father would be the one to consider! Even to this day, I don't know Razmi's exact relation to my family. I had heard two different versions from my mother: "Razmi's mother was my Grandfather's step-sister" and "Razmi's mother was my grandfather's cousin, *dokhtar daii.*" I'm still confused!

My curiosity to figure out why my grandfather periodically wired money to Razmi—based on very old wire receipts and letters that my father had meticulously kept and I discovered after his death—allowed my imagination to run wild and think maybe a little hanky-panky was going on between my grandfather and Razmi's mother! Well, that would make a good juicy story from 100 years ago!

My grandfather had financed Razmi's education and had advised him to attend Darolfonoon—a modern university at the time. Instead, Razmi preferred the army and had gone to military college. He had joined the army and, for a while, he was stationed in Azerbaijan, the Turkish-speaking province in northwest Iran. At some point, he must have reached the rank of colonel.

Based on bits and pieces I heard from my father, Razmi had connections with a rebel group that had planned a coup against Reza Shah (father of the later deposed Mohammad Reza Pahlavi, Shah of Iran). But the coup had failed and the rebels were defeated and hanged, and Razmi was blacklisted. "He was lucky to be alive," I heard my father say on several occasions about Razmi. However, he was never promoted beyond the rank of colonel, and then was forced to retire. I never saw Razmi in military uniform. As far back as my memory permits, he was retired and lived in a big house with a beautiful flower garden, somewhere in the northern part of Tehran, near Shemiran.

He definitely was a fun-loving guy. He stood a little over five feet tall, and was rather skinny, with black-rimmed glasses, thinning gray hair, and a loud hearty laugh. Razmi always struck me as a bit of an old romantic. Looking at him, or listening to his conversation, I sometimes sensed his nostalgia and longing for the years gone by. When he was stationed in Tabriz (capital of east Azerbaijan province) he had married a young girl—short, plump, fair-skinned, beady blue eyes, and frizzy light brown hair. I called her Aunt Mary. She was Razmi's second wife (I heard this bit of information from my mother). Who his first wife was, I have absolutely no idea!

The Razmis had no children of their own. But Aunt Mary had a niece and a couple of nephews who hung around. The caretaker of their vast property, who resided in a small cottage at the end of the premise, had several little ones. Plus they had a couple of big dogs. So there was an ample venue for them to channel their love and affection, and satisfy their emotional needs.

Razmi was a chain-smoker and a heavy drinker. I also heard he was a womanizer in his younger years. On many occasions I heard him say: "It is sinful and a waste to be buried ten feet under with perfectly healthy organs: liver, kidney, and heart!"

He sure used all of his organs to the max and lived to be over ninety years old.

Visiting Razmi's house during the Persian New Year, *Norouz,* was pure agony for me. Aunt Mary was a good cook and was excellent at baking. She made candies and cookies from scratch during the New Year, while my mother always bought the traditional sweets. Aunt Mary displayed her mouth-watering products on a long table along the wall of her living room, apart from the rest of the furniture. On that table she usually had cakes made with pistachio and yogurt; candies made with honey, slivered almonds, and saffron; and small delicate cookies made with chickpeas and rice flour decorated with poppy seeds. But Persian etiquette dictated we not help ourselves to these goodies unless they were offered. The problem was Aunt Mary never offered. I needed strong self-control not to touch or taste the goodies. I have no doubt the seeds of my love for sweets and my intense desire to learn how to bake were planted in Uncle Razmi's living room.

Razmi had a great sense of humor and was truly a fun person to be around. Once when I was twelve years old, the Razmis came for dinner. Suddenly, he challenged me and Homa on a bet,

"I bet you I can wear your mother's white jacket inside out, walk outside to the nearby store, buy a packet of cigarettes, and come back," he said.

Homa and I giggled and said it would never happen—that a man of his stature would never wear a woman's jacket, particularly inside out, and go out in public.

Razmi said we could follow him on his mission and watch what he did, with one stipulation only. We were not to get close to him or laugh. He did precisely what he said he would do. He looked absolutely ridiculous. He walked into a corner store and, with a straight face, looking directly at the cashier, asked for a packet of cigarettes.

The attendant didn't know what to make of this distinguished, serious-looking old gentleman in a woman's attire. He didn't dare to laugh but kept gazing at the jacket. Razmi suddenly looked bewildered, bent his head, and looked at what he was wearing. With a tinge of surprise in his voice he declared, "Ha, in the dark I couldn't see what I was putting on. I'll be darned."

With that said, he picked up the cigarettes, paid, and calmly walked out of the store. The poor cashier was still gawking at him with a half-opened mouth.

Homa and I lost the bet!

The Razmis were tight with their money. The extent of their generosity was the occasional opening of their house and garden to relatives to come and have a picnic on the traditional day of picnicking and outings, *seezdeh bedar,* which occurred once a year, thirteen days after *Norouz*. Of course, families brought all the food and drink. Despite their affluence, I never received any Persian New Year gift from them. Once Aunt Mary promised to make me a doll, but it never materialized.

Razmi was an educated man and knew French and English. On many occasions he corrected my pronunciation of the words that began with the letter V or W, and the distinction between the two. They also had some Armenian friends with whom they celebrated the western New Year.

The Razmis were frequent visitors to our house and often stayed for lunch or dinner, which makes me believe my parents must have enjoyed their company. I had ambivalent feelings towards Razmi, as I never felt any emotional connection to him as a close relative. However, his flamboyant character certainly intrigued me.

29

Light of the Era

S he referred to her husband as "The Prince." I saw this so called "Prince" only once when I was seven years old. He must have been a descendent of the old Qajar dynasty, the ruling family before the Pahlavi's. She came for tea accompanied by "The Prince," whose actual name was Ebrahim Mirza. He was a military officer and looked old, tall, and thin. He chain-smoked and probably even used opium on a regular basis because of the yellowish color of his skin and the nasal tone of his voice.

The way she catered to this old man, and always interjected her talks with "the Prince said this or the Prince said that" clearly indicated she was proud to be married to him. According to family reports, the old Prince was given a new position in another city; while there, he took a second wife! Mother always said the reason for the second marriage was because he wanted children. But he was unable to produce any offspring even with the second wife. Except for that one time, I never saw the old Prince again.

But we saw plenty of her. My father addressed her as *Ammeh Khanoom,* "Lady Aunt". I believe my father was her grandnephew. This old Aunt, who was known to us as *Forough Zaman,* "The Light of the Era", was a permanent fixture in all family outings and gatherings.

Forough Zaman didn't have any children of her own, but she considered herself the matriarch of her brother's family who had three kids. They all catered to her whims and wishes, and actually they all lived in her huge house; she was a woman of means.

The Light of the Era was witty and amusing with a dreadfully foul mouth. With her piercing brown eyes, wrinkled olive-colored skin, long loosely braided black and white hair tossed over her shoulders, she was capable of delivering her nasty remarks like bitter candies wrapped in colored paper, as well as pouring insults like sprinkles on cupcakes. And everyone laughed!

The amazing part was that no one took offense to her remarks. Even more amazing was her understanding of never picking on the little guy. Her remarks were directed towards the powerful and well-to-do. The higher the position and stature, the more she picked on the person and handed out insults.

Like a caricature artist, Forough Zaman's remarks exaggerated certain unpleasant characteristics of an individual in a hilariously insulting way! Characteristics that others had noticed, but never acknowledged or dared to comment on. Because of her old age, she was immune from any retaliation.

At Uncle Razmi's annual picnic, Forough Zaman usually walked in yelling, "Razmi, you bastard stingy son-of-a-bitch. Where are you hiding your money?"

Everyone roared with laughter! So did Razmi with a loud belly laugh.

This Light of the Era passed away when I was a teenager. My memories of this fun and quirky lady are associated with picnics at Razmi's gardens, beer, accordion music, singing, dancing, Persian food, and an abundance of insults delivered with merriment.

30

The Ritual at the *Hammam*

If I mention to my grandchildren that I did not wash myself until I was in my teens, what would their reaction be? But it is the truth; I did not wash myself, I was always being washed.

The ritual of going to *Hammam,* the Persian bath/spa, was unique. Each neighborhood had two or three *Hammam.* Actually, my best friend's father, who was a businessman, owned a *Hammam* in our neighborhood. Mother accompanied me when we went to *Hammam.* She always asked for a specific *dalaak,* wash lady. Her name was Ozra and she must have been in her twenties.

We would arrive, having reserved a private stall; we undressed in the dressing area but kept our underpants on. We then walked into the hot area where there was a platform to sit on. A few minutes later Ozra would arrive. She was chatty, fun, and really good and thorough in washing me.

First she would wash my hair two or three times. She used the green soap that Mother brought along. I didn't care for its smell. It was made with olive oil and my father always bought the bars wholesale in boxes. Ozra was gentle when washing my hair and massaging my scalp. My hair then was rinsed with warm water and it felt good and squeaky clean.

The part I didn't care for, because it tickled and was uncomfortable, was when she applied *sange pa* to my feet. It was a chunk of black, pumice stone that she rubbed on my heels to smooth the skin and remove any callouses I had.

Then came the ritual of exfoliating. Ozra used our *kisse,* a coarse mitt—also brought from home—to remove dead skin. I liked Ozra because she was gentle; I had other wash ladies prior to Ozra who practically skinned me alive! The final stage produced a soft lacy cloth bag, with a draw string, which contained a little soap inside which made lots of lather and bubbles—and I liked this part—that covered me from head to toe. Then I would stand under the warm shower to rinse the soap. This was my favorite part and I usually lingered more than necessary. But Mother never objected.

My mother paid Ozra directly. Probably that was her tip, because she also paid the *Hammam* manager separately. This ritual was repeated every week.

When my dad sold Grandfather's house and we moved (I was 12), the new house had a shower, and I didn't go to *Hammam.* I didn't mind since Ozra had left—she had married and was gone. I never asked for another *dalaak,* and began washing myself!

31

Aunt Tooran

Aunt Tooran, three years older than my mother, was a teacher and not married. She was stunningly beautiful—she was known as the "pretty lady" in her Tehran neighborhood. I was her first niece; she spoiled me and I loved it. I'm told my mother breastfed me until I was almost a year-and-a-half. When it was time to wean me from breastfeeding, Aunt Tooran took me away for a few days, and I guess after that I did not suck on my mother's breast any longer!

Aunt Tooran had a best friend named Behjat—I assume they both taught in the same school. When I was about five years old, Aunt Tooran and Behjat took me to the Boat Club.

The Boat Club was similar to a small amusement park but had a man-made lake in the middle of the park with little boats that people could ride for fun. Auntie and her friend and I were in one boat—but I recall we were not alone. Some young officers were in another boat and they were all splashing water at each other, giggling and having a grand time. When the boat ride was over, one of the young officers invited us to have something to eat in the Club. We stayed there pretty late, and by the time we returned to Behjat's house, where we were spending the night, it was way past midnight. By today's standards that is nothing, but seventy years ago, in Tehran, it was frowned upon for two young beautiful women to stay out that late. On the way home I was instructed not to say anything to Behjat's mother—she had no father.

The next morning at breakfast, Behjat's mother lashed out at the girls. She was very angry and was scolding them for staying out late— whatever else she was saying did not make sense to me or I did not understand, being so young.

A month passed by and I never mentioned the Boat Club episode to my parents—I was not supposed to. Then one day, while riding on a city bus with my parents and Auntie, I saw the same young officer from the Boat Club sitting behind my parents. I recognized him and smiled at him. His face was void of any reaction or indication of recognition. I turned to my aunt and opened my mouth to say something but met her glossed-over eyes; she did not even turn her head to the direction I was pointing. I must have been smart enough at that early age to immediately recognize the gravity of the situation and quickly shut my mouth. No one said anything after that.

Dating and going out with young men was an absolute taboo in those days and was not a socially accepted behavior. At the Boat Club, Aunt Tooran and Behjat had been defying all the social rules and having a good time. That is why Behjat's mother was so furious.

Several years later, Aunt Tooran got married. She lived to be ninety-one, and in her old age she was just as pretty, jovial, and fun-loving as when she was twenty-one!

32

Aunt Ashraf

Aunt Ashraf ("Ashi") was my mother's younger sister. For as long as I remember, these two sisters had a stormy relationship. Periods of being nice and civil to each other were followed by longer periods of not talking to one another.

I didn't care how these sisters treated each other. I liked Ashi, and when I was old enough to visit relatives all by myself, I made sure to drop in periodically for visits.

Aunt Ashraf and I shared a love for sweets. We both had a sweet tooth somewhere in the mouth! When I visited her, I was certain there would be an assortment of pastries, cookies, and cakes. Only one time that I recall she did not have any sweets to eat after lunch, so we improvised. Mixing cocoa powder with sugar in a small bowl quenched our cravings for a piece of chocolate after the meal.

Ashraf had married at the age of seventeen and her husband was eleven years her senior. I have a vivid memory of what happened during a family gathering. A large group of relatives were picnicking at a ranch on the outskirts of Tehran. Grownups were having a good time with plenty of food, drinks, and music. Ashi's husband was a heavy drinker at the time. He almost passed out in the bathroom and ended up with a ghastly cut on his shin. Because he was so drunk, he was unaware of the pain. As a seven-year-old kid, I was observing it all, and was eavesdropping on family gossip. Rumor had it that in addition to his drinking, he also had encounters with prostitutes. His behavior agitated Ashi and made her terribly upset, hence their constant fights.

But then suddenly—and I don't know why—he made a complete turnaround. They said it was the influence of his older brother who was a pious and religious man. Aunt Ashraf and her husband made a pilgrimage to a religious shrine in Karbala, Iraq, and when they came back they were both transformed and were totally different people. He did not touch another drop of alcohol, and my modern Aunt Ashi opted to wear *hejab,* and cover herself from head to toe in *chador.* He had embraced the fanatical side of Islam, and she had willingly yielded to wearing the *hejab.* I assume she must have reasoned that as long as he did not drink and did not have extra-marital sex, it was worth paying the price of covering herself in public.

Their relationship flourished and they ended up with six children. Because of the brood, my aunt seldom accepted dinner invitations—it was such a chore for her to tote along six little ones to any relative's house.

It baffled me that Ashi's husband considered himself such a staunch Muslim by embracing foolish doctrines. What he believed to be Islamic had no resemblance to what I had learned about Islam from my parents. He blindly followed advice from some fanatical friends, such as: Don't buy pastries from the Armenian bakery because the baker was not Muslim!

One summer afternoon I was visiting Aunt Ashraf. She sent her maid out to buy pastries for our afternoon tea. The maid came back with a huge box, holding an assortment of yummy-looking French style pastries.

Ashi's husband looked at the box and barked at the maid by saying, "Didn't I forbid you from buying pastries from that Armenian bakery?"

No one knew what to do or say at that time. Delicious-looking pastries were winking at six little kids, and he himself was unable to hide his cravings.

"Okay, let's go ahead and eat," he said harshly. "But you all go and rinse your mouths afterwards."

I just sat there with an open mouth, bewildered as to where in the Quran it is mentioned that eating pastries from a bakery owned by an Armenian is a sin! Did my aunt really believe this stuff? I didn't think so.

Another peculiar version of his Islamic belief was the ban on using television. But of course they had one—how else could they keep six kids entertained? But in order to get a good reception, they needed an antenna. He had insisted the antenna be installed behind the house, out of the sight of his Muslim friends. As told by Aunt Ashraf, it turned out his so called "religious buddies" all had televisions, with antennas also in the back of their houses. What a façade!

Ashi's husband smoked heavily—religion did not ban smoking—and he ended up dying of a sudden heart attack at the age of 50. Many years later, Ashi came to California and lived near one of her grown daughters. I kept in touch with her and once reminded her of the pastry episode. She sure remembered the incident and we both had a good laugh about it over the phone. Sadly, she died of ovarian cancer.

33

My Honorary Title

Despite his authoritarian parenting style, my father was most respectful in his language use when I was growing up in Tehran. My parents never used profanity; they never called me names; and they never belittled me with words. Equally, respecting my parents—regardless of my childish anger and outbursts at times—was an important part of my upbringing.

In my early years, admittedly, I was a stubborn child, with episodes of throwing tantrums now and then. I had my fair share of being spanked and disciplined. There were times when my father tolerated my unruly behavior. However, if my insubordination had not raised his anger to a boiling point, he would then simply put me down by calling me an "Uzbek." So, I grew up believing an Uzbek was someone with bad behavior.

Remembering that sometimes I was called an Uzbek as a child, I was determined to find out who an Uzbek was, and why I was one at some point in my life. A bit of research clarified this mystery.

I began my research by going through the internet. The information I found under Facts and Details regarding Uzbekistan and its people added to my knowledge. There are over thirty million Uzbeks who live in Uzbekistan, and my father had identified me to be one of them at some point during my childhood. Uzbekistan is north of Afghanistan and Afghanistan shares a border with Iran on the east side. Then why was I an Uzbek when I had never set foot in that country?

Apparently Uzbekistan is the most ethnically diverse country in Central Asia. The Uzbeks are an ancient Iranian people that intermingled with nomadic Mongols and Turkic tribes. The word Uzbek probably comes from two Turkic words: *vz* and *bek* which means "Genuine man." I also read somewhere that the word Uzbek or Ozbek means "real," "original," or "true."

Voila! The mystery is solved, and I have a perfect explanation. Whatever I did as a young child to make my father grant me the honorary title of "Uzbek," I must have been downright "original."

Map & Photos

Family Tales
from Terhan

وفات مرحوم تغفور وجنت مكان لما ميرزا غلام محسين ولد

كل بابابيك دائر لما ميرسيد محمد طبا طبائى بتاريخ

My grandfather: Gholamhossein, son of Golbaba Beik.

Grandfather (seated) with his two sons, my father Hassan (left) and Uncle Jafar (right). Standing: Agha Baba, the butler (center), and his assistant.

My father Hassan (left) and Uncle Jafar (right) in their early teens.

Uncle Jafar (left) and my father (right) were two brothers with love, respect, and admiration for each other.

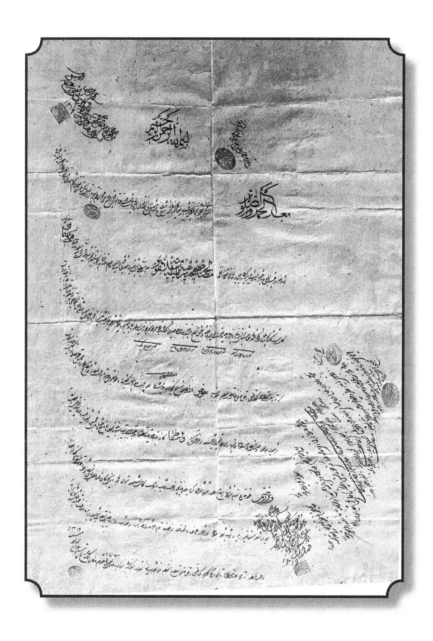

The deed to my grandfather's house on Bouzarjomehri Avenue, near the Big Bazaar. This document is more than 100 years old.

Cousin Manooch was my childhood buddy. He was a year younger and I was an inch or two taller.

The Golbabai brothers – Uncle Jafar (left) and my father, Hassan (right). It always felt like having two fathers.

Manijeh (left) and Homa – I always considered her as an older sister. Homa was my father's cousin.

Homa became a math teacher and received recognition for the work she had done.

A rare photo of Aziz, my father's aunt as a young woman (right), and her only daughter, Homa. They were part of our family.

Below: Manijeh in 5th grade.

Above: Khaleh Joon and my father. I thought of her as a truly liberated woman in a male-dominated society, more than a half century ago.

I'm 2½ years old in this photo. Perched on top of snow in the middle of the courtyard with the persimmon tree.

Mother in her younger years – she was a beautiful woman.

My mother in May 2013, three months before she passed away. She was still beautiful in her old age.

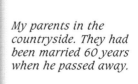

My parents in the countryside. They had been married 60 years when he passed away.

Above: Agha Baba, the old butler, visited us when I was very young. Homa and I with the two brothers who were very fond of Agha Baba.

Left: Young Razmi in his military uniform. I still don't know his exact relationship to my father.

Part III

My Trips
Back to Iran

My Trips Back to Iran

When my father passed away in Tehran in 2001, I had been living in the United States close to forty years. I attended his funeral and the anniversary memorial. In his will he had named me the executor of his estate, and that is when my frequent trips back to the old country started. The subsequent ten trips were for the sole purpose of assisting my mother: going over my father's papers and clearing his study; donating his books to the local library; organizing Mother's finances; taking care of the house maintenance; attending to Mother's health and medical needs; and, after she passed away twelve years later, preparing the house for sale.

As an executor, I had the responsibility of making sure all my father's wishes—which he had clearly spelled out in his will—were properly executed. Making these long journeys, taking time off from teaching, and dealing with issues and bureaucracies in Iran were all part of the deal.

During all these trips, I kept notes of events and activities. After each trip, I congratulated myself for the tasks I had accomplished. Stories in Part III deal with my memories of this period. After my father's passing Mother made five trips to the United States, but ultimately preferred to be in her own home in her own country, and I respected her decision.

Mother passed away in 2013.

34

A Phone Call

The phone rang at two o'clock in the morning. My mother's quivering voice at the other end said, "Your father is in the hospital." She was trying not to cry. I thought to myself it must be more serious than that, otherwise she would not call in the middle of the night to tell me Dad was in the hospital.

"Mom, please tell me the truth. What is wrong?" I sounded composed and serious.

"He is gone. Your father is gone," and then she began to cry.

I could hear muffled noise and voices in the background. It must have been mid-afternoon her time in Tehran. My mind went blank and I could not think of anything to say at that moment.

"You are the eldest daughter and need to know," she continued. "Tell me what to do. Should we go ahead with the burial right away, or wait till you get here?"

My parents lived half way around the world. The fact that I could not take off right away to attend my father's funeral was a reality. I had to check my passport, arrange for a plane ticket, and notify my employer.

I tried to calm Mother down and gently told her the truth.

"Mom, I cannot think right now. May I call you back in a few minutes with my answer?" She understood and agreed for me to call her back.

I hung up the phone in the dark. Sitting up in bed, I hugged my knees in absolute silence in the middle of the night.

In the Islamic tradition, burial must take place as soon as possible. The ritual of mourning a loved one is done in several stages. On the third day, the seventh day, and the 40th day after the passing, family and friends gather to mourn the deceased. I don't know the significance of these particular days, but I was sure that I could not make it to Tehran on time to attend the third day services.

After ten minutes I picked up the phone.

"Mom, please go ahead with the burial and I will try to make it for the seventh-day-memorial service."

"Will you call your sisters and let them know?'

"I will Mom, as soon as the day breaks."

Going back to sleep was out of question. I paced the floor back and forth. I walked every inch of the house by going downstairs, to the basement, back up again—not doing anything but just thinking.

I felt numbness all over my body. I kept thinking of my monthly conversations with my father over the phone. During the past year-and-a-half, each phone call had ended with him reminding me that "his time was up" and that I should be prepared to hear the news of his passing! On several occasions he just wanted affirmation that he had been a good father. And many times I had confirmed that indeed he had been a good and wise father.

I had resolved my own feelings as an adult child and reached the conclusion that despite his authoritarian parenting style, he really had my best interests at heart. He was always a serious man, but towards the end it was easier to make jokes and keep the conversation on the lighter side. When he kept talking about dying and repeating that his time was up—he was 83 years old at the time—I would joke around by saying, "Well, Dad, after all no one got out of this world alive."

Now he was gone, quickly as he always wanted. A massive heart attack in the morning and gone by early afternoon! All I did after my mother's phone call was to remember our monthly phone conversations. I did not cry.

Three days later I was on the plane to Amsterdam. Joined by one of my sisters, we arrived in Tehran in the early morning hours four days after our father's passing.

Entering the house, walking into my father's study—where Mother had kept the door shut and the light on—I felt his presence. Still I did not cry!

I sat in the swivel chair near his desk, and glanced at the top of his desk. Everything was as he had left it: books; notebooks; writings; pieces of paper here and there with handwritten notes, some in ink, and some in pencil.

Absent-mindedly I picked up a piece of paper. It appeared to be a poem he had copied. I read it, and then read it a second time. Suddenly the meaning hit me! It was a poem by Rumi, the Sufi Persian Poet.

Let us appreciate one another now,

Lest we are parted suddenly.

Wise men treasure their friends,

Put aside meanness; we are humans.

Unkind thoughts darken friendship,

Let's get rid of those dark clouds.

Would you be happy when I'm dead?

If you befriend me after I'm gone,

You would feel the sorrow for the rest of your life,

Then imagine I'm dead now, come let's be friends.

If you come to kiss my grave someday,

Then come now and kiss my face,

I'm the same person.

That is when I realized my own peace and serenity stemmed from the fact that I appreciated him while he was alive, and I had told him so.

35

The Final Memorial

Traditionally in Iran, the ritual of mourning a loved one occurs in several stages. Families observe four memorials in honor of the deceased: on the third, seventh, and fortieth days after the passing, and the final one on the first anniversary of the death. I am only able to attend one of the first three—my father's seventh-day memorial.

Now a year has passed, and Mother has been reminding me of the important upcoming annual memorial celebration. She wants all three of her daughters to attend. This is the final ritual after which Mother stops wearing black and starts wearing colorful attire—and I assume will go back to coloring her hair again. For the entire year she has been wearing black.

I and my sisters decide to make the trip, and arrive in Tehran a few days before the memorial.

Attendance at this memorial service is by invitation. She invites relatives, neighbors, and close friends. The event takes place on a Friday, the holy Sabbath. It is a whole-day affair. Mother knows exactly how she wants the memorial service to be conducted.

She puts a relative, Pejman, in charge of the arrangements and expenditures.

Pejman is a dedicated young man and trusted by my mother. She hands him a large sum of money and he is to pay the bills and keep track of the expenses. They have chartered a bus to take the attendees to and from the cemetery. They have arranged for the rental of 100 chairs, many small tables, tea glasses with silver holders, and additional serving dishes. They have ordered a fresh flower wreath and have hired two male servants to work in the kitchen and serve guests tea, juice, pastries, and fruit.

Even if I disagree with some of these arrangements, I will not object to what Mother has planned. She has it all figured out and has a clear picture in her mind of how she wants the memorial service to be. My two sisters and I have been away from the country for so long that we no longer are familiar with the protocol and the customs. It is best to follow her tradition.

Two days before the event, her neighbor, Sara, comes over in the morning. The two ladies make halva together. It is a tedious and labor-intensive work. Equal amounts of butter and flour are stirred constantly over low heat until the flour turns golden brown. Then a syrup made of sugar, water, ground saffron, and a bit of rose water is poured into the browned flour and stirred until it is completely absorbed. This sweetened cooked dough resembles the consistency of Play-Doh. It is then shaped or flattened on plates, decorated with slivered almonds and pistachios, and given to the recipients that my mother has in mind. Halva is delicious and a familiar staple at funerals and memorials.

Mother and Sara make two large batches of halva. It takes them more than half a day to accomplish this task. They bicker and argue over the amount of flour and sugar for each batch. I am an observer, but help with the stirring once in a while, and leave the two ladies to do their job. They are good friends and certainly know what they are doing.

My two sisters and I do our parts: we flatten the first batch onto several oval-shaped plates, using the back of a large spoon. We use our creativity to decorate the plates of halva with slivered almonds and pistachios.

These plates are earmarked for the employees of the local bank, the neighborhood grocer, and the construction workers who are working on the renovation of a nearby building. This is a close-knit neighborhood; businesses, shop owners, and residents all know each other. I deliver them all, with specific instructions from Mother to ask the recipients to say a prayer for my father's soul.

The day before the memorial, Pejman and one of the hired men come over in the morning to remove or re-arrange furniture in my mother's house—they have to make room for the rented 100 chairs and small tables! They leave only two bedrooms intact, but haul the rest of the furniture to the large and long balcony and into the third bedroom.

The delivery van arrives in the afternoon with the chairs, and all the other stuff Mother has ordered. With the help of the hired man—whom we have come to know well because he was also present at my father's funeral the previous year—we arrange the chairs the way Mother wants them in the living room and family room. By 11 p.m. the work is done and the stage is set for the memorial service the next day.

One of my sisters and I share a queen-size bed in my father's old study, which Mother has now re-decorated as a bedroom. Despite being very tired, we are unable to sleep. We toss and turn for about an hour and then decide it is useless to stay in bed.

We get up and quietly tip-toe into the kitchen. There is work to be done: baskets of oranges, tangerines, apples, small cucumbers, and a lot of kiwi fruit are to be washed and readied for the fruit arrangements to be served the next day. Soon the younger sister also joins us. We work on the second batch of halva. We make tiny halva sandwiches by putting a spoonful of halva between two thin wafers. These are to be served at the graveside ceremony tomorrow.

Despite our whispering and being quiet, Mother also wakes up. She objects to the work we are doing and says, "There will be nothing left for the male servants to do tomorrow!"

We know we have to be up by 7 a.m. and need to get some sleep. The past two nights we have been able to sleep with the help of Tylenol PM. Fearing we might oversleep, we do not take any pills this time and luckily manage to get a couple of hours of sleep.

It is Friday and the day of the memorial. The guests who will be riding the chartered bus to the cemetery arrive at 8:30 sharp. The bus is ready and parked on the main street. The flower wreath made of white gladiolas with a big black bow on top of it is attached to the front of the bus—I suppose as a symbol that the bus is headed for the cemetery.

By 9:30 a.m. the loaded bus takes off for the southern part of Tehran, toward Behesht-e Zahra Cemetery. Some folks opt to drive their own cars and follow the bus.

I see relatives and cousins on this bus whom I have not seen in forty years. I exchange greetings and pleasantries with them all. The road to Behesht-e Zahra goes through a very busy section of Tehran. However, being a Friday, when most shops are closed, the traffic is lighter. By 10:30 we arrive at the cemetery, which is a small city all by itself. We enter through a designated gate. Already there is a long table and several chairs set up near my father's grave. Trays of halva in round thin wafers, orange juice, dates stuffed with walnut, bottles of water, and disposable cups are all on the table.

I'm anxious to see my father's tombstone. Last year, after my father's funeral and before I left Iran, my mother and I ordered the headstone. It is a beautiful, large rectangular piece of green granite. Mother purchased the plot for the two of them, and the tombstone is large enough for two sets of engraving.

I am curious and ask Mother about this idea of being buried together in the same grave, like a double-decker bus! Her response shuts me up: For the duration of his life, your father was always on top of me! After I pass, I want to be on top of him!" Okay Mom, no further questions asked!

Mother, my two sisters, and I kneel down by my father's grave. The rest of the folks are either standing or sitting on the chairs, arranged a few feet away. The large gladiola wreath with the black bow is now off the bus and laid on the tombstone.

A man, hired in advance, begins reciting verses from the Quran. He has an excellent singing voice. The weather is perfect this morning. Due to a bit of rainfall the previous night, all the evergreens, flowers, and the tombstones have a shiny fresh look. The weather is cool enough which makes wearing a long coat and black scarf rather comfortable. The serenity and the prevailing sadness in that place, combined with the singing of the reciter, stirs up my emotions and I start crying quietly.

Suddenly a loud noise startles me. A few yards behind our gathering, another memorial service is taking place. That family has opted to have a bugle player for their service—one who plays loudly, rather off tune, and disturbs the peace in the surrounding area! While our man is still singing and reciting the verses, and the bugle player is carrying his offbeat noise, I can't control myself and start laughing. The whole episode is so comical. With my head down, dark sunglasses, and the black scarf covering almost half of my face, no one can see my range of emotion! Fortunately, it is the end of recitation, and shortly thereafter the bugle player quits playing. The noise stops and calm prevails. It is the end of the graveside memorial. I gently bend my head and kiss my father's grave, well-aware that all eyes are on us.

The bus is ready to take the guests back to a local restaurant for lunch. Mother has made the reservations way in advance. On the way back I sit up front, next to the bus driver. Realizing that I have been out of the country for a long time, the driver takes pleasure in explaining where we are and mentions the names of the streets prior to the Islamic Revolution. Old names bring back memories, but I do not recognize any of the streets. Tehran has changed, too.

It is half past noon when the bus stops in front of the restaurant. The guests are all invited to have a traditional Persian meal of kabob, rice, yogurt, salad, bread, and tea. Chicken kabob is also available for those who do not eat meat. Except for two couples sitting at the far end of the restaurant, we have the whole place to ourselves. Our guests sit where they please, in groups of four or six.

Mother orders some take-out meals to be delivered to the local grocer and his crew. Pejman, who is in charge of the whole operation, keeps counts and makes sure all the guests receive proper meal and hospitality. I believe he pays for 80 lunches. God bless Pejman who is like a son to my mother. My sisters and I are not familiar with all the traditions, and are not of any help at this time.

We know the in-house memorial reception will begin at 5:00 p.m. Some folks depart from the restaurant and go home, planning to come back to the house later. Others, who have longer distances to travel, opt to come to Mother's house and linger until the reception begins. They are mostly my father's cousins, relatives, and a few of Mother's friends.

We are back in the house by 3:00 pm and after a heavy meal, it is siesta time! The two male servants have arrived, and are busy in the kitchen, brewing tea and arranging fruits in platters to put on the small glass tables. The two bedrooms left intact are unique sights to behold. I look through my mother's bedroom door and see four ladies stretched alongside each other on the king-size bed. A few are snoozing on the Persian rug on the floor. I open the door to the bedroom that my sister and I share and see my father's old cousin and her family, including her grandkids, are all milling around. I stay in the kitchen, drink tea, and chat with the two hired men.

A beautiful flower arrangement—also ordered by Mother in advance—is delivered. She puts it on the dining room table with two black candles on each side. The sweet smell of tuber roses, known in Persian as the Maryam flower, fills the place. The rest of the halva, stuffed dates, and Danish pastries are all on the tables.

At exactly 5:00 o'clock a new singer and reciter of the Quran arrives with his assistant, a microphone, and two amplifiers. The house is packed with people: relatives, neighbors, and friends. He begins by reciting verses from the Quran, then talks about the deceased (my father) and then, based on the information he has been handed, he mentions us—the three daughters—by name and rattles off our educational backgrounds and degrees we have earned. Then he begins to sing again. The microphone carries his voice out into the street. The front door to the main building is wide open for people to come and go. The guests are offered tea and orange drink. They sit wherever they please. All the women are wearing black scarves and some cry softly. It is a sad and somber gathering. When his task of singing and recitation is over, he stops and invites the guests to go ahead and enjoy the fruits that are before them on glass tables.

Suddenly an old friend of my father springs up to his feet, grabs the microphone, and starts eulogizing my father. This comes as a surprise to everyone. Totally unplanned! He is a good orator and talks about different seasons in life, indicating that he himself is in the winter of his life. He talks about my father and in general delivers a nice and sweet eulogy for fifteen minutes. I appreciate his speech and clap at the end. But I'm the only one who does it, so now all eyes are on me. They probably think I'm strange! Well, it is okay if I make a fool of myself, these people will not see me again!

Later on I learn the fifteen minutes overtime use of the microphone costs Mother extra money. But she doesn't mind.

By 9 p.m. the guests are gone and only close family members and relatives remain. Mother has the supper ready. I can't believe it—she has been cooking and freezing for almost a month.

"When people are here, one must have food ready to feed everyone," she says. And indeed she does, lunches and dinners.

I'm absolutely exhausted—it has been a very long day!

The following day by 2 p.m. the rental agency has picked up the chairs, tables, and the extra dishes. Mother's furniture is put back in its original place, and we are all ready to crash and do nothing. Pejman and his wife—my cousin, Marjan—show up with two videotapes. We eat supper, change into our pajamas, and sprawl in front of the television watching two Persian movies until 2 a.m.

The memorial celebration is behind us and Mother is happy and satisfied that it was done in style, upholding her deceased husband's stature in the neighborhood—the final memorial celebration.

36

Homa

It is 2014. I come home to find a phone message from my cousin, Marjan, who lives in Tehran, notifying me that Homa has passed away as a result of a stroke. This is an extremely sad news, yet I feel comfort in the fact that I made the effort to visit her in Iran in 2007 as related below.

Homa was my father's cousin. She and her mother, Aunt Aziz, lived with us in Grandfather's big house. I considered her as an older sister. She was in her sixties when she passed away.

It was a difficult task to get my mother on the train from Tehran to Shahrood. That is where Homa lived, roughly 250 miles west of Tehran. I wanted to travel alone, but Mother insisted on accompanying me. Our original plan was to spend one night in a hotel, visit Homa and her family, and take the train back to Tehran the next day. But Homa would not hear of it; no way would she let us stay in a hotel.

I met her husband, her son, and her daughter-in-law at the train station for the first time. Despite her extreme shortness of breath and difficulty breathing, Homa had insisted on coming to the station to greet us. When I saw her in the waiting room, I broke down and cried. She had aged a lot and gasped for air when she talked. Obviously there was something seriously wrong with her lungs. It was a short taxi ride from the station to her house.

As long as I remember, Homa was never a jovial person. She seldom laughed and rarely displayed signs of happiness or an enjoyment of life. I guess Aziz's old-fashioned ideas and superstitious beliefs were permanently instilled in Homa: don't laugh, if you do, something bad and nasty will happen. I had heard that myself from Aziz many times.

Homa had the same disposition when I visited her in Shahrood. She had burned her left hand a week or two earlier from hot oil on the stove. She had said nothing to her family at the time. Instead, she had poured salt on the burns! When her family found out, they had taken her to the hospital for proper medical care and dressing of the wound. She had her own way of dealing with problems in life and, despite her education, some of Aziz's fanatical beliefs were deeply ingrained in her. As if she truly believed this world was only for suffering!

Homa never took medication and once I asked her why. She replied pills did not agree with her. For an educated woman, a smart mathematician, she appeared ignorant of certain aspects of life. It was mind-boggling to observe the extent of Aziz's influence on Homa's upbringing. Although we grew up in the same household, and she called my father *Agha joon* "Dad"— indeed he was like a father to her—somehow Aziz's words carried more weight, and were deeply rooted in her. No wonder my father, who loved his old aunt, Aziz, and took care of her, was always clashing and arguing with her over Homa's upbringing.

While at her house I took pictures of the citation letters by the ministry of education recognizing her as an outstanding math teacher.

That afternoon of my visit—when the rest of the family took naps—I sat next to Homa and we had a private conversation in low voices. Just the two of us.

Not having an actual father had profoundly affected her—something I had never realized. Although she called my father *Agha joon,* and I always regarded her as an older sister, she had felt totally abandoned and rejected. It was then that I realized how hard it must have been for her to grow up in our house!

"Did Dad ever punish you physically?" I asked her bluntly, because I had been subjected to corporal punishment myself as a child.

"Never," she said and I believed her. Dad would have never raised a hand against a fatherless child.

My father and Uncle Jafar did a lot for her: making sure she finished teachers' training college. They paid cash to buy her a little house near where she taught so she and her mother, Aziz, could live independently. By then Homa was earning a salary and could take care of her mother.

Homa did pay them back for the house. I recall Dad had a separate ledger for Homa. Every month, she came over and paid something to Dad, which was then recorded in that ledger. It was like paying for the house on installment—except there was no interest added. Houses were bought and sold based on cash and not bank loans.

Homa took care of her mother and didn't get married for as long as Aziz was alive. By then I was living in the United States and didn't know much about what was happening back home. After Aziz passed, Homa was all alone. Her good neighbors found her a husband, a retired tailor who lived in her neighborhood. She was in her mid-forties by then. Since she could not have children, due to the removal of her ovaries, she gave permission to her husband to take a second wife for the sake of getting a baby. The result was Reza, the good-looking young man I met at the train station with his cheerful, smiling, cute young wife. Based on family reports, Homa raised the baby. So Homa is the only mother he knows. Whatever happened to the other woman, I don't know and no one ever shared any information with me.

Homa retired as soon as the baby was born; she sold her house in Tehran and moved the family to Shahrood. Occasionally, I heard my father comment that it was a good move on Homa's part. She bought a nice house in a small city; one with fresh air, plenty of countryside, and away from the traffic madness and pollution of Tehran.

Mother and I had to take the train back to Tehran. We barely had enough time to take a taxi tour of this quaint small city and shop at its bazaar.

It was a memorable visit—we talked, cried, reminisced about the past, and I got to meet Homa's family. What a treasure that trip was!

37

A Sudden Trip to Iran

The phone rings at 5 a.m. It is my cousin from Tehran. After the customary pleasantries, she gets to the real reason for her call,

"Auntie has overdosed on her medication. She must have taken two days' worth of pills in one day by mistake. Her doctor has made a house-call and she is okay for now. But she no longer can be trusted to live by herself. You must come and do something."

"How could that be?" I ask. "Zoe left just two weeks ago. What has happened within these two weeks?"

My youngest sister, who lives in Los Angeles, had spent seven weeks with Mother in Tehran.

"I know!" replies my cousin. "But you are the only one who can make rational decisions about Auntie."

Good Lord! I cannot just drop everything and travel overseas. I have commitments, not only to my school, but also for a speaking engagement I had agreed to almost a year ago. Briefly, I explain to my cousin it is not possible to take off right away and travel clear across the world. She understands and says for the moment the neighbors are taking care of my mother.

"But it is really essential for you to get here as soon as possible," she emphasizes.

Within ten days I leave for Iran.

After a long flight, going through Frankfurt, I reach Tehran and am at my mother's front door at 4 a.m. Mina, a temporary caregiver, opens the door. My cousin has arranged for Mina to spend the nights at my mother's. I'm exhausted but I cannot sleep. As soon as we eat breakfast, Mina leaves. The neighbors breathe easier—the responsibility has shifted now that I have arrived.

There is no time to get over my jet lag. Mother looks older and smaller than two years ago when I last visited her. She has no recollection of the events of the last two weeks. She brushes off all my questions and says "It is nothing important. Everyone gets sick now and then."

She is glad to see me, but insists she is fine and that I didn't need to make the trip for her sake! She indicates she can take care of herself, and does not recall the medication overdose, the often-burnt food, and the dangerously high blood sugar.

What am I supposed to do with my 87-year-old mother, and what choices do I have? I spend a week to acclimate myself, to re-enter the culture, and to observe. I talk less and listen more. Every bit of information helps me to formulate my thoughts.

I think of three options: I can bring her back with me to the United States to live under my roof, or I put her in a nursing home in Tehran. The third option is for her to stay in her own home and I arrange for daily in-home care. Unfortunately, when I gently describe these options to Mother, none is acceptable to her. She wants to stay in her own home but does not want in-home care. She says she does not need one.

I'm patient and observant. She can still take a bath by herself, but slowly. She can still cook, though often burns the food. She is diabetic and is remiss in taking her blood sugar. When she is by herself, she does not eat properly. She has also developed a moderate dementia. Everyday I listen to the same old stories and laugh at the same jokes that she repeats over and over again.

I decide to pursue my three options simultaneously and am determined to make decisions based on what is best for my mother, not what is convenient for me and my sisters. For the first option, I go ahead and renew her passport and get all her travel documents in order. For the second option, I begin visiting available nursing homes. For my third option, I get the name and phone numbers of agencies that provide in-home care.

After visiting a few nursing homes in the area, I determine my mother does not belong there—at least not at this stage in her life. I bring up the topic of her coming back with me to the United States. She says she can no longer make this long trip and prefers the comfort of her own home. I don't blame her. As time goes by, I realize she is indeed correct. She loves her home and knows how to function in it. I want the best for her, and this is the best.

Now I need to provide her with in-home care. Unfortunately, Mother had an unpleasant experience with in-home caregivers after her heart surgery. She tells me about missing stuff, and believes the caregivers stole from her. Indeed, people I consult with, regarding in-home care, warn me to be careful and I hear horror stories of dishonest caregivers. How do I find a trustworthy person?

I spread the word among friends and relatives to let me know if they hear of a reliable caregiver. Lo and behold, a friend calls with good news. A woman who had taken care of an elderly gentleman with Alzheimer's for nearly two years is now available. The old gentleman has passed away and the woman is looking for new employment. The family vouches for the woman's integrity and honesty.

I call her up immediately. She comes over the following day for an interview. She is 61 years old. In the course of a couple of hours she tells us her entire life story. She is a retired educator with a retired husband at home who has Alzheimer's. An unemployed son and a five-year-old grandson also live with her. She needs to work. When she tells me how long it takes her to get to my mother's house, I'm flabbergasted. She lives too far away. She is knowledgeable and well-versed in health care areas. She wants to work from 8 to 4, which suits Mother well. We agree on a salary and a four-day trial period. I want to observe how Mother reacts to having her in the house.

Mother, who is quiet and polite during the interview, is vocal and belligerent after the woman leaves. She steadfastly repeats she does not need anybody's help. I keep calm and remain nonchalant, "Let's try her for four days, it doesn't hurt," I say smilingly.

The next morning, the caregiver shows up ten minutes early. She and Mother cook together in the kitchen. I deliberately leave the house several times, buying vegetables and dairy products. During the day, the caregiver talks about her family problems, her misfortune, and the tough life she has had. Her stories are not cheerful and I'm concerned about the effects of such negative and sad conversation on Mother. Four o'clock rolls and the woman is out the door. Mother sounds like a broken record, "Get rid of her. I don't need anybody."

Oh God, please tell me what to do! I pray.

The second day of the trial period is here. The caregiver brings some personal items such as a few changes of clothing, a book of crossword puzzles, a book of poem by Hafez, her personal medication, calcium pills, and a jar of Vaseline. I ask her to use a couple of drawers in the spare bedroom to store her belongings. She definitely wants to settle in. Today, Aunt Tooran and her daughter also show up for lunch. Mother is still unwilling to accept this person. I'm at my wit's end. I do not have the heart to dismiss this woman who obviously needs the job. On the other hand, Mother is not cooperating, and is very unhappy. I hardly sleep that night. I meditate, cry, and pray in the solitude of my bedroom for a solution. I ask God to help me.

It is the third day of the trial period. It is past 8 a.m. and the caregiver has not arrived yet. I'm not worried, considering the distance and the traffic. But when there is no sign of her by 8:30, I decide to call her house. I dial her number. The grandson answers the phone. "Hello, is your grandma home?" I ask.

"My grandma is dead," the five-year-old boy answers.

For a split second I think maybe the young boy is mad at grandma for leaving him at home, and that his words are the expression of his anger. I cannot think straight.

"Can I talk to your father?" I say bewildered and shocked.

The son picks up the phone. I introduce myself, and quickly ask if his mother has left the house. The young man begins to cry at the other end.

"We lost my mother. She is gone. She is dead."

I am numb and feel as if a bucket of ice water is dumped over my head. Then I begin to cry as well.

"How did this happen? We were together the day before, ate lunch, and watched a movie on television," I manage to say in broken sentences.

"She was hit by a car, taken to the hospital, and died in a coma," he says sobbing.

Mother comes out of the kitchen holding a box of tissue. I no longer know what to say and am pinned to the sofa. I ask the son if I can go over to their house and take back his mother's personal belongings.

In this part of the world, people strongly believe in fate and the will of God. Did God take the decision out of my hands? Was it her fate to get hit by a car? Why would God want this woman to die? Why did I meet her?

There are no answers to any of my questions. But I ask again: "God, what do you want me to do now?"

38

Finding a Caregiver

I am desperate to find a caregiver for my mother. She won't be coming back with me to the United States and I can't stay in Tehran indefinitely. My husband, family, and job are all in another continent. God, please help me to find a solution to this problem!

Words of my father come back to me, "Keep your connection with a higher power. It doesn't matter where you pray—in a mosque, a synagogue, a church, or in a Buddhist temple. It is all the same."

His words have been ingrained in me. I need collective wisdom. I pick up the phone and call the home of a local Ayatollah. The 90-year-old Ayatollah's place of residence is only a few blocks away. He holds religious classes and folks go to him for counsel. Maybe he can solve my problem.

The old Ayatollah is a pleasant, calm, attentive individual. I explain the situation and ask if he knows of any trustworthy local person who would be willing to be my mother's caregiver. He asks a series of questions: mother's age, how heavy she is, her financial situation. I notice he asks the same question a couple of times—and I repeat the same answers. I wonder if the old Ayatollah is having a mild dementia. He says he will get back with me.

Two blocks north of my mother's house is a synagogue. I'm in need of a place of worship. The local mosque, which is of equal distance from her house, is closed. So I head for the synagogue. It is a Saturday morning and as I approach the place I see a woman and her young daughter going in. I join them. In that synagogue all the ladies walk upstairs and the gentlemen stay downstairs. I sit with the young woman and explain that I don't live in Tehran but am visiting my mother for the time being. We chat. A few minutes later a beautiful woman with a heavily made-up face, well-dressed with fine jewelry, walks in and sits in our pew. She keeps looking at me. So, I feel obliged to introduce myself.

"I'm from the United States and am visiting my mother who lives on 11th Street," I say with a smile.

"Which house? I also live on 11th Street," she asks with curiosity.

When I tell her the house number, she looks surprised and with raised eyebrows says, "You are Mrs. Golbabai's daughter—I didn't know her daughter is......" and she stops her sentence midair.

I know, she thinks I'm Jewish!

I smile and just say, "I'm in need of a place of worship to connect with God."

She relaxes and smiles back. I pray again, "God what am I supposed to do?"

39

Kismet

I look up and this time ask the divine power vehemently, "God, what DO YOU want me to do?" But there is no reply.

It is Monday, March 21, the beginning of Persian New Year, *Norouz*. The Iranian calendar registers the year 1390 (2011 Western calendar). It is a time for celebration, joy, and gift-giving. But I'm not in a happy mood. I cannot feel the excitement and the jubilance felt by the neighbors, relatives, and the rest of the population in Tehran.

Two days ago, the caregiver I was about to hire for my mother was hit by a car and died. Off and on I cry for this woman whom I hardly knew—but of course I don't let Mother see my tears. People go about their business and everyone is shopping like crazy, preparing for the arrival of the New Year.

Mother instructs me to order cookies from the local pastry shop. Since I'm doing the shopping, I buy what I like: small rice cookies with poppy seeds on top and round almond-filled pastries. Inside me, however, I feel the turmoil. None of the neighbors react the way I have reacted to the death of this woman who was to be my mother's caregiver. They all believe her death was the will of God—that it was the woman's fate. The tragedy befallen the caregiver's family is difficult for me to accept. I try to console myself by repeating that when in Rome do as Romans do! I must convince myself that it was her destiny.

In the neighborhood where my mother lives there is an abundance of stores with a variety of goods and services. I hardly ever leave this neighborhood to shop anywhere else. Banks, restaurants, groceries, bakeries are all within a short walking distance, even a mosque, a synagogue, and doctors' offices. I know the owners of these businesses and I'm sure they know who I am, too. An American friend who had visited my mother several years ago told me Mother's neighborhood reminded her of places in New York City.

My usual cheerful disposition has changed to somber and pensive. I cannot smile, and cannot forget the death of the caregiver. I'm terribly worried. What if I cannot find someone to take care of my mother? I cannot stay here indefinitely. I stop at the local green grocer to pick up the assortment of fruits my mother has ordered for *Norouz*.

Ali Agha, the owner, has been in the neighborhood for the past 45 years. He took over the business after his father passed away. He knows my family well—actually he knows everyone in this neighborhood. He is a pious, watchful, and family man. At times, it appears he treats everyone like his own family. On several occasions he and his brother have discussed their children's education with me, have shared their kids' adolescence problems, and have asked for advice on certain issues. Immediately he notices my changed disposition.

"What is wrong? Is your mother okay?" he asks.

"Yes, she is fine," I reply without smiling

"Is your family in the United States all healthy? Your husband, son?" he inquires.

"Yes, they are all fine," I say without looking at him.

"Then what is the matter?" he persists.

I break down and tell him about the caregiver and the fatal accident. He quietly utters a short prayer and then asks:

"What type of caregiver are you looking for? Daily or 24-hour?"

I explain that Mother is not at the point of needing 24-hour care, but she does need daily supervision—someone to administer medication, make sure she eats, and take care of light household chores.

Ali Agha thinks for a moment and asks how much I'm planning to pay such a caregiver. I repeat the numbers the agencies had quoted me when I inquired about daily care. At this point, Ali Agha rubs his chin and says, "Let me check something; I might have just the right person for you."

I thank him, pay for the fruit, and leave the store.

It is March 27 and we have had a steady stream of visitors: relatives, neighbors, and friends who come for the customary Norouz visit. On this particular afternoon, a relative of my father and his wife plus their four grown children show up. I do not know them well. I'm gracious and repeat all the necessary greetings and pleasantries.

The phone rings and it is Ali Agha at the other end. "There is a lady here, the one I told you about. Could she come over and visit you now?" he asks.

"By all means!" I reply.

In a few minutes, the woman recommended by Ali Agha is sitting in my Mother's living room. She is poised, graceful, nice-looking, well-dressed, and terribly uneasy and shy. Mother makes no objection and sits through the visit—we treat her like a friend visiting—I bring her tea and offer cookies.

That evening in the solitude of my bedroom I praise God and thank Ali Agha for sending her to us. She is about fifty years old, lives only a few blocks north of my mother's, has two grown children in college, her husband is dead, and she needs to work. Apparently, she had asked Ali Agha to find her employment with a good and respectable family. Ali Agha, with his keen knowledge of the folks in his neighborhood, puts our two requests together and recommends this woman to us, a better fit than any agency could make. Ali Agha's recommendation weighs a lot, and I respect his judgment. The woman starts work the next day.

I have a little over two weeks to show the new caregiver the ropes, get to know her, and observe Mother's interaction with her. I don't hear any objections from my mother except for comments such as,

"Why pay someone when there is hardly any work around here."

I chuckle because while I'm here, Mother's life has been organized, food and medication served on time, shopping and cleaning done! I'm doing all the work!

"I know Mom." I say laughingly. "You don't need anyone to do your housework. But I will have to go back soon and you need a companion, someone to talk to and to gossip about me!" We chuckle.

By mid-April I'm back in the United States!

We are now taking one day at a time. I call my mother almost daily and speak with the caregiver, in private, once a month, to answer her concerns and questions. I've made arrangements with a friend to pay the caregiver's salary away from my Mother's house and out of her sight, as she still believes it is a waste of money to have someone come to the house! For the time being, Mother sounds happy and content. She tells me her new companion is nice but is not going to stay long as she is looking for a job. Mother thinks the caregiver is there because she is out of a job and doesn't have anything else to do but to come and keep her company! I chuckle. Whatever works!

It is hard to believe I trusted the care of my mother to a person recommended by the local green grocer. But there are unwritten, unspoken cultural practices in that part of the world that are hard for us to understand in the United States. One thing, however, is certain: the problems of old age and parental care are the same in any culture and don't recognize geographical boundaries. For now, I must believe in *kismet,* or fate.

40

Meeting a Taliban

It is 2009 and I'm visiting my mother in Tehran. I meet two young men
from Afghanistan who work in Tehran. One power washes the exterior of
a building near my mother's house and the other one does menial home
maintenance for Aunt Tooran.

We are having lunch at Aunt Tooran's place. She has three darling
small dogs that yap as soon as someone approaches the door. I
feel a bit congested and am wondering if I'm allergic to dogs. After a
delicious but heavy lunch, my mother, Aunt Tooran, and her daughter
are ready for a siesta. They nap while I stay in the family room and read.
Once in a while I check on the two little canary birds kept in a cage in
the kitchen. By 5 p.m. the rest of the family is up from their nap and are
ready for an afternoon tea and some ice cream!

It is 6 p.m. and Mother and I are ready to go back home. We call for a
cab but are told there is a 40-minute wait time. It is the busiest time of
the day to find a cab.

While we are waiting, the doorbell rings. A young, slender young man
named Saeed walks in. I learn he is from Afghanistan and periodically

does some home maintenance work for my aunt. He appears to be in his twenties, clean-shaven, and speaks Farsi with Afghani accent.

While my cousin is getting Saeed a cup of tea, I decide to ask him a pointed question.

"Saeed, who are the Talibans?" I ask with a smile.

"I'm the Taliban," he replies, sounding surprised.

I proceed to ask more questions, and he has no qualms answering them. I find out his parents and sisters are from Kandahar but are now living in Herat. He and his older brother opted to come to Iran to work, and they send money back to Afghanistan to their parents.

I ask him why the Talibans are fighting the Americans. And this is exactly what he says, "Because America wants to destroy Islam."

"How much education do you have?" I ask nonchalantly.

"None. I can only read the Quran, but I cannot write," he replies.

"Do you think your sisters need some education to read and write?"

"No, just to be able to read the Quran is enough," he says.

"Why don't you think it is necessary for the girls to have some education?"

"Because they get married," he says. "They take care of the husband, house, and children. They don't need to work. The husband will provide for them."

Then he adds with a smile, "If somebody provides for me, I'll be happy not to work."

"Is it true you buy your wife?" I ask casually.

"Yes, we have to pay a sum to the girl's parents to secure a wife." He mentions the amount.

I calculate the sum to be close to $13,000, based on today's exchange rate

"Don't you think it is a little too much to pay for a wife?" I add nonchalantly! "I saw another Afghani young man the other day who was washing a house in my neighborhood and he said he had to pay $4,000 to the girl's father."

"Yes, but the type of wife I want costs a lot more," he boasts. "You get what you pay for."

Then he thinks a bit longer and adds,

"There are also some who don't cost anything."

"What do you mean?" I ask, very surprised.

"Like when a boy and a girl like each other and decide to get married."

I want to continue the conversation and get more insight into Saeed's life and his goals, but the taxi arrives and we have to leave.

So, this is what a Taliban looks like!

41

Visiting the Family Doctor

It is fall of 2009, and I'm vising Mother in Tehran. For the past two days I've had a sore throat.

Despite gargling, taking Tylenol, and using other home-remedies, I'm not getting better and tell Mother that I need to see a doctor. Her old family physician, Dr. M, has moved to a new office only a few blocks from Mother's house. Occasionally, he also makes house calls.

Mother calls him at home to find out what time he would arrive at his office! "At 9:00 o'clock," she is told. I ask my mother to give me the address so I can go by myself.

"No, I must accompany you. Besides, I have some shopping to do in the vicinity."

To get Mother ready and out the door is time-consuming and a major accomplishment. But she insists on coming along. While she is getting ready, her neighbor, Sara, walks in. To her, my sore throat is the catastrophe of the century!

"Should I make you some soup?" Sara asks with an alarming voice. "Let me come to the doctor with you. God strike me dead—I should burn some *Esfand* for you (to fight against the evil eye that has caused my sore throat). Bad eyes, evil eyes—that is what has made you sick."

Sara says all these quickly in one breath. By now, I have lost my voice and try to whisper and can't reply to her phrases of sympathy.

By 9:45 we are finally out the door. The doctor's office is only a few short blocks north of her house, but Mother insists on getting a cab. We get into the cab and Mother says, "Dr. M's office should be around here."

I have learned that my mother knows places by sight and never has an actual physical address. The cabbie is good-natured and starts looking at the buildings to see if he can find a sign with Dr. M's name on it!

"Now, we have gone too far. Let's get out and walk south," she says to me.

We get out of the cab, and within that short distance she makes two inquiries, one from a guy at the newsstand and one at a nearby pharmacy. Both point to the same direction. That is good news—we are on the right track.

Dr. M's new office is on the second floor of a building. Three other doctors practice in the same area. He greets us as we walk in. He is an old gentleman, short, trim, and speaks with an Azari (Turkish) accent. As I sit in his office, I look around and notice his diploma—doctor of medicine from Tehran University—the date on the certificate catches my attention; he graduated before I was born!

Dr. M is gentle, kind, very slow, and methodical. He takes my temperature. Then he cleans a metal tongue-depressor with alcohol—it looks like a shoe horn—turns on a lamp and looks inside my throat, both sides are extremely tender. He checks my glands and takes my blood pressure, twice. Then he frowns.

"Your blood pressure is too low for your age," he says.

"How old do you think I am Dr. M?" I ask half smiling.

"Forty-one or forty-two," he replies.

I can't help it and tell him he is such a sweetheart for making my day! Then I tell him, "I'm sixty-five years old."

"How long have you lived in the United States?" he asks.

"Over forty years," I reply.

"Well, come and stay here for a couple of years, then you will age properly!" he says with a chuckle.

He prescribes antibiotics, cough syrup, and a "cold pill" which I assume is antihistamine for keeping the nasal passage open.

Then it is Mother's turn to be checked by Dr. M. He takes her blood pressure and starts lecturing her on reducing salt and avoiding anything made with shortening, and emphasizes the benefits of walking. For every advice he gives, Mother has a counter-excuse for not following it! He reviews her medication and renews some pills.

Our official visit is over and now Dr. M starts talking about my father. He says they were kindred spirits and used to exchange books. Like my father, he is also interested in history and philosophy. He says he has given away most of his books, but is keeping the ones he really likes, such as Will Durant's *History of the World.* We talk and exchange pleasantries until there is a knock on the door—another patient has arrived. He spends 45 minutes with us.

His fee, based on today's exchange rate, turns out to be $7.50.

42

A Day at the Park

Park Shafagh is a few short blocks from my mother's house. I love this park—not only is it an oasis in the middle of a busy neighborhood, but also it was my father's hangout in his final years of life. I understand he walked there often, met with his cronies, discussed world affairs, and, I like to think, maybe he also enjoyed a game or two of backgammon. Whenever I visit my mother, an early morning walk through this park is a must for me. Not only does it give me the exercise I need, but a walk also allows me to think and meditate in order to find solutions to the myriad of difficult situations I face.

Today, I take my camera and head for the park at 7:45 a.m. More exercise equipment has been added since a year ago. I see a ping pong table, a badminton court, swing sets, walkways, a round pool with a fountain, benches, and of course the cozy library to which my father's books were donated. Backgammon and chess tables are available throughout the park. There are also exercise groups for men, women, and one for mixed genders. Last year I joined the ladies aerobic group for a while, and it was fun.

This morning three gentlemen are doing their morning exercise routine. I ask if it is okay to take their picture. No objection, so I click the camera.

Nearby, on a bench, I see an old gentleman sitting quietly. As I walk, I encounter women in *chador,* young girls in scarves, all walking briskly getting their daily exercise. I walk around the park and when I come back, I see the same old gentleman still sitting on the bench. I approach him and ask for permission to take his picture. He is very pleasant and invites me to sit down next to him.

"How come you are not walking or exercising?" I ask with a smile.

"I can't; I have heart problem and the doctor says I should only walk very slowly," he replies with an Azari (Turkish) accent, smiling broadly.

I ask a few questions about his heart condition, and then ask if he wouldn't mind telling me how old he is.

With a smile he says, "In some foreign countries, they say if one dies before 80, then one is a loser. If one dies after 80, one is a winner. Let's say I'm still a winner!"

I like his sense of humor. He also takes a liking to me and volunteers more information about himself. He had been in the field of communications when he was young, *mokhaberat.* Then he proceeds to tell me the following story—maybe as a joke:

> "Mozaffar al-Din Shah (from the Qajar dynasty) meets Napoleon, and asks him why Napoleon has only one wife. He replies: because we run the country through laws, and not through Harems."

He then laughs heartily! He is on a roll, and tells me another story—I'm not a historian and don't know how true his story is:

> "Naser al-Din Shah Qajar wanted to get rid of Amir Kabir, his capable prime minister. He orders Amir Kabir's death by sending an assassin to Kashan, where the prime minister was exiled. The hit man finds Amir Kabir in a *hammam* (spa) and tells him he is about to die, and then produces a variety of poisonous potions. But Amir Kabir prefers his artery to be cut. While he is bleeding, he tells the assassin to take a message back to the King: *Tell him I cut his artery sixteen years ago.* The message is relayed

to Naser al-Din Shah. He is baffled and asks what is meant by that message. They report back to him that sixteen years ago Amir Kabir established "Darolfonoon" a modern university and institution of higher learning in Persia, to enlighten and educate the young. Educated people don't buy the rubbish from the throne!" and then he chuckled and continued, "So the King orders Darolfonoon to be closed—but it was reopened later on."

The old man finishes his story. We both understand the meaning of his story and what he is trying to convey.

"Do you think people are educated enough these days?" I ask.

"Some are and some are totally ignorant."

He laughs again. We both understand what he means. He is really on a roll now. He tells me another story:

"Once upon a time, during the Ottoman Empire in Turkey, there was a religious leader who was unkind to his people. His name was Hamid and he wore a turban. He banned his people from naming their kids Hamid, because he wanted to be the only Hamid. People were fed up and revolted and got rid of him. The day he was gone, not a single man with a turban could be found in the streets of Turkey."

Again, we both laugh out loud, and understand the meaning of his story.

All the while he is talking, he is also trying to get rid of a piece of chewing gum stuck to his pants.

"When you get home, maybe a bit of vinegar or alcohol would help you get rid of this gum," I suggest—not sure if I'm correct.

I take a closeup photo of this pleasant old man and leave the park.

In my subsequent visits to the park, I never see him again.

43

A Trip to Qom

M r. Atashi is a friend of Ali Agha, the green grocer. He also owns his own car and runs errands for special clientele. Mother uses him when she wants to take short trips. In essence, he acts as my mother's chauffeur.

Today we are going to the holy city of Qom, about 140 kilometers (87 miles) south of Tehran—this will be a whole-day trip. Qom is the center of religious learning for the Shia sect of Islam, with Islamic seminaries for the pursuit of advanced religious studies. Many ayatollahs have studied in Qom. It is also a place where folks pay respect to the Shrine of Fatima Masumeh. It is also the place where my mother's parents are buried.

Mother tells me that when she was a little girl, her father was the chief of police in Qom and a close friend of the governor. Subsequently, when he passed away, he was buried in Qom. My grandmother, who had moved to Tehran after her husband's passing, wished to be buried in Qom as well. That is why my mother and Aunt Tooran visit that city at least four times a year, to visit their parents' graves and pay respect to the Shrine of Masumeh.

Aunt Tooran and a friend of my mother, Mrs. K—whose mother is also buried in Qom—accompany us on this trip. The ladies show up at our house prior to 8 o'clock in the morning and, shortly thereafter, Mr. Atashi arrives, ready to drive us four ladies to Qom.

Mother has prepared lunch for all of us the night before. They don't like to eat restaurant food while in Qom. We will have chicken sandwiches, fresh fruit, hot tea, sweets, and bottled water for our midday nourishment in Qom.

With the exception of one stop, we drive straight to Qom, and arrive in the downtown area by 11:30. Because it is a religious city, wearing a scarf is not enough—we must wear a *chador* on top of the scarf in addition to the ankle-length robe.

We are all wearing our scarves and ankle-length robes, but before we leave the car, we must put on the *chador* as well, a big piece of fabric that covers us from head to toe.

I look out the car window and see nothing but a sea of black *chadors*. I look at our *chadors,* and they are breezy cotton with colorful floral patterns! To be able to put on a *chador,* and get out of the car in sweltering heat at the same time, requires extreme dexterity and maneuvering. Somehow we manage and step onto the sidewalk. All eyes, including young and old clergy with black turbans, are on us. We are wearing large sunglasses, trying to hold on to the *chador* with one hand—it does not entirely cover our bodies—and hold on to our bags with the other, and walk toward the well-known Qom Bazaar. We stand out like four sore thumbs, or as I would like to think of it, as four lovely colorful flowers in a field of black. It is obvious we are not local.

Mrs. K has knee problems, my mother and Aunt Tooran walk at a snail pace, it is high noon, it is close to 90 degrees, and we are wearing all those covers. I'm sweating like a pig. Mr. Atashi announces that he is parking the car in the same spot and will wait for us until we are done shopping. Mother says we will be back in half an hour! Given the slow pace of the ladies and the length of the bazaar, I'm bewildered. But I'm a guest and do not question the miscalculation. Our procession slowly heads for the nearest entrance to the covered bazaar. Suffice to say, two hours later we are still in the covered bazaar. Knowing Mr. Atashi is waiting for us, I volunteer to walk fast and let him know the ladies are on their way.

I find Mr. Atashi standing by his car, near the curb. We wait together for 10 more minutes, but there is no sign of the ladies. I trace my steps back into the bazaar quickly, but there is no sign of Mother and the other two ladies. Thinking they might have used a different exit, I re-route myself, walking quickly, and get back to the car. There is no sign of them.

I repeat this a second and third time—I'm attracting attention.

"Are you looking for a lost child Ma'am?" a merchant asks. Apparently there is a lost kid somewhere in that bazaar.

"No Sir. I'm looking for three lost grown ladies! They were on this spot ten minutes ago."

I say this with no smile—I'm hot, tired, and rather cross!

I get back to Mr. Atashi. He looks at my red-beet face covered with sweat, the scarf, long robe, and the *chador,* and suggests I stay put and he will go find them. Five minutes later he comes back with good news. He has spotted the floral *chadors* in a place which is the total opposite of where the car is parked.

Following my mother's instructions, Mr. Atashi drives us to the location of a private mausoleum. It has a quaint courtyard with rooms all around. An old guard rushes to greet us and hurries to unlock one of the rooms. To me, this room is like finding a stream of cool water in the Sahara Desert—a ceiling fan, Persian rug on the floor, a table, and six folding chairs. We quickly shed all the covers.

Mr. Atashi joins us for lunch. I casually mention we have brought a lot of food, more than we can eat. "The day is not over yet, we might need a mid-afternoon snack," my mother reminds me.

A little rest and relaxation after lunch and the cool air, via the ceiling fan, gives us energy to get up and follow the afternoon plan. We are going to the Shrine of Masumeh for prayer and meditation.

We leave our shoes with two ladies who place them in cubicles and then walk into the Shrine. An absolutely magnificent sight greets me: walls of mirrors that look like a kaleidoscope, white columns, colorful Persian rugs covering the entire area, and women sitting on the floor engaged with their own prayers and meditation. Some are reading the Quran. A few are stretched on the floor, apparently napping. They have total freedom to do as they please in that cool and beautiful place of worship.

Aunt Tooran and Mrs. K begin their prayers. I sit quietly and watch the people inconspicuously. Then I spot a young, good-looking woman in a corner with a bunch of books spread in front of her. She is studying something. Curious as to what she is reading, I slowly move closer to her. She is reading a text for her English class and is working on the exercises. As an English teacher, my curiosity is peaked. I must talk to her.

We have the most delightful conversation and I'm pleased that she welcomes my assistance in completing her exercises. One of her assignments is to write down the different types of music: classical, country, jazz. I ask her if she has ever heard of Elvis Presley and the rock and roll music. No, she has not. She adds rock and roll to her list to discuss it further with her teacher.

"Can I meet with you again here at the shrine tomorrow?" she asks.

"No, actually I'm visiting Qom for the day."

And then I add, "I'm visiting the country only for a few weeks."

I do think about this young lady sometimes, and wonder where she is today.

44

The Iranian Art of Negotiation

The year is 1993 and it has been twenty years since I last saw my parents. I make a hasty two-week trip to the country of my birth, Iran. My parents are getting old and my father is sick. He is in bed during my entire visit.

I'm overwhelmed by all the beautiful hand-made rugs I see in relatives' homes and inquire whether there are any restrictions regarding purchasing a rug to take back to the United States. I'm not sure what the government regulations are these days, because after the revolution many things have changed. The answer is affirmative, but I am permitted to take only two pieces out of the country.

I don't know how to buy a rug, and of course my father, the great negotiator, is sick in bed. He calls his trusted friend and asks him to assist me with the selection of an appropriate rug. His friend, charged with this important mission, does not want to act alone. He, in turn, calls his own brother who is a rug expert.

We all meet in the morning at the rug gallery of Mr. Asadi, the rug merchant, somewhere near the center of Tehran. While he shows us rugs of different qualities and sizes, he also plays the role of a gracious host by offering us tea, fresh fruit, and bowls of delicious Persian ice cream.

Trays of freshly brewed tea in tiny glasses keep coming around and Mr. Asadi's workers keep displaying rugs for our inspection.

Two hours pass and, based on the recommendation of my father's friend, we select six pieces. Mr. Asadi says he will personally bring the rugs to my parents' house so that my father can examine them as well.

Up to this point, no one has mentioned any price. I'm feeling very nervous. The two expert gentlemen calm me down by saying, "First like the rug, don't think of the price."

I remember their own comments while looking at different rugs: "this is a pretty one," "that one smiles at you," "this rug really grabs you."

In late afternoon, Mr. Asadi delivers the rugs to my parents' house. This time, it is my mother who plays the gracious hostess and offers goodies to Mr. Asadi. He consumes several cups of tea along with some pastries and a bowl of chocolate ice-cream. His earlier hospitality has now been reciprocated. We push aside the little coffee tables in the large living room. Mr. Asadi spreads the rugs in the middle of the room, slightly overlapping. My father manages to get out of bed, and, still in his pajamas, comes and sits on the sofa next to his friend, the rug expert. He nods approvingly and sanctions the quality of the rugs. Now comes the big moment; they begin talking price.

The "art of negotiation" which my father practices flawlessly and with perfection has always fascinated me. I pay careful attention to his every word and watch his every move. I don't want to miss anything—maybe I will learn a few lessons. We refer to it as "bargaining," but it is truly an art which combines carefully chosen words, gestures, movements, and psychological connection. It requires "know-how" and flair.

Mr. Asadi smiles and announces the rugs have no value compared to his friendship with my father! Dad looks at him affectionately, smiles back and says, "Go ahead Asadi, give us a price."

After a few moments of hesitation to show his reluctance, he finally utters some numbers.

My father's friend is holding a notepad and a pen. Upon hearing Mr. Asadi's figures, he scribbles something on the paper. He and my father bend their heads together while glancing back and forth at the rugs and the notepad. After a few minutes of consultation, in low voices, Dad's friend turns to Asadi and calmly asks, "Do you know how to subtract?"

Mr. Asadi smiles from ear to ear and replies, "But I'm much better at addition!"

Again, my father and his friend whisper. This time they write down some numbers and push the paper in front of Mr. Asadi. Suddenly, the smile is totally wiped off Mr. Asadi's face. He takes a look at the numbers and simply says, "Don't even bother. These rugs are my gifts to you. No payment is necessary."

By this time, even I get the drift—the offer is way too low for him to even consider it.

The negotiation continues for almost an hour, until they mutually agree on a price. In the meantime, fresh cups of tea keep coming out of my mother's kitchen. Mr. Asadi is having a great time visiting, socializing, and doing business all at the same time. My father is negotiating and purchasing in the privacy and comfort of his living room. Of the six rugs on display, they select two and set them aside, and the rest are returned to Mr. Asadi's car.

As an observer and the recipient of the purchased rugs, I'm fascinated by the whole process. The language, gestures, facial expressions, and unspoken understanding displayed by both parties are something to behold. Above all, neither party feels cheated. There is a mutual satisfaction that indicates a win-win situation for all.

45

How to Purchase a Persian Rug

A family friend once advised me, "Don't buy a Persian rug unless you fall in love first." He meant with the rug! Purchasing rugs in Iran is a unique personal experience. It is an emotional odyssey combined with lessons in sales, marketing, and the art of negotiation. I went through it all when I went shopping with my mother in Tehran.

On that memorable day, my mother was up early and kept repeating, "We've got a lot of work to do today."

She was clearly anxious for us to get an early start on our shopping. She had called Mr. Asadi the day before to let him know that we would be visiting his rug gallery. Mr. Asadi is a rug merchant and a long-time friend of my family. He said he would be glad to pick us up in the morning on his way to his rug gallery. Mr. Asadi lived only a block away from my mother's house. His place of business was roughly a fifteen-minute drive; however, with the incredibly congested traffic in the city of Tehran, it could very well take almost two hours or more to drive the same distance. To be equally kind and gracious, Mother invited Mr. Asadi to come and have breakfast with us prior to our visit to his gallery. He was delighted and accepted my mother's invitation.

Mr. Asadi showed up at 8:00 o'clock in the morning. I had not seen him in several years and was rather amused to see him in a red and white Hawaiian shirt. He looked trim for his age, which I guessed to be in the late 60s. He had gone slightly bald and was wearing glasses. He joined us for breakfast at the kitchen table.

Freshly brewed tea, butter, home-made quince jam, my mother's favorite cheese—more like cream cheese than feta—a bowl of apples, two kinds of flat bread, and a container of yogurt were all placed on the kitchen table when Mr. Asadi arrived. Being an early riser, I had already eaten my usual breakfast: a bowl of natural yogurt, topped with quince jam, and one apple. But I did join them at the table and had a glass of hot tea.

It was almost 10:00 a.m. when we reached Mr. Asadi's gallery. One of his sons, Mohammad, a good-looking young man in his early 30s, greeted us with a huge smile at the entrance of the gallery. We all spent ten minutes exchanging greetings, pleasantries, and inquiring after each other's family health. Four other young men in the gallery were performing various duties; two in particular were in charge of displaying the rugs for prospective buyers.

As soon as we entered his gallery, Mr. Asadi whispered some instructions to one of the young men who immediately dashed out and disappeared in the street. In less than ten minutes he was back with a box of pastries. Another young man brought a tray of freshly brewed tea in short glasses and placed them in small round saucers. I chuckled, as we had barely finished breakfast. However, to my own disbelief, the appetite was there, and I easily managed to enjoy a couple of pieces of pastry followed by a glass of hot tea.

I looked around the gallery with admiration and amazement. Colorful hand-made rugs were on display everywhere; some were stacked on a pile, others were uniquely displayed on the walls. A few rugs made of silk were so delicate that they were framed like paintings. It was overwhelming to think they were all made by hand, knot after knot. I felt joy, pride, and excitement. Too bad I couldn't buy them all—they were truly exquisite.

My daughter-in-law had commissioned me to buy her a rug, preferably one with a terracotta color scheme within a certain price range she could afford, as some of these rugs could cost several thousand dollars each. Alas, indicating a certain price range is not how one buys a Persian rug!

I remembered the advice of the rug expert who said I must first fall in love with the rug, "It has to grab your attention, and you must tell yourself this is the one you want to live with and look at every day," he had emphasized. "The rest is secondary."

I kept looking around, anxiously awaiting the moment when a rug would cause my heart to leap out of my chest. The young men at the gallery flipped open the first pile of rugs, one after another. Mr. Asadi brought a few more rugs from the back and spread them on the floor, close to the huge glass doors of his gallery. I knelt down and ran my fingers gently over them, admiring the workmanship. But even touching and caressing these rugs did not produce that certain "heart palpitation."

We were offered another round of tea. Then an older couple walked in. Mr. Asadi knew the couple and rushed to the front of the gallery to greet them. They waived their hands and said they just wanted to look around. I thought to myself, "Maybe they are also looking for love at first sight." A second pile was being flipped open for the couple. Now I had two piles to look at. Suddenly, from the corner of my eyes, I caught a glimpse of that certain reddish-brown color my daughter-in-law had in mind.

"Hold it right there!" I told the young men.

Expertly and gently, they pulled out the rug from under the pile so that it was in my full view. I felt like a suitor sizing up a future bride. Wow, it was indeed beautiful and unique. They kept referring to it as the Pazyryk rug, a replica of an antique design made in Tabriz. Mr. Asadi rushed to his back office and brought out a book on rugs. Sure enough, there was the history of the Pazyryk rug, the oldest surviving carpet, dating back to 5th century B.C. It was discovered in the 1940s at Pazyryk in southern Siberia. The original piece, whatever is left of it, is now hanging in the Leningrad Museum. It was magnificent, with a field of squares in the middle, and a border displaying fallow deer, horses, and lions. Excellent! I asked Mr. Asadi to put the Pazyryk rug aside, and didn't even ask how much!

In the meantime, the elderly couple looked at a few rugs and left the gallery. Obviously nothing had grabbed them. By now, a nice-looking, middle-aged woman entered the gallery. She was just hanging around and looking at different rugs. She seemed to be knowledgeable about rugs and appeared to be a regular visitor at the gallery. Mrs. T, as I learned later, was a businesswoman who imported merchandise from Europe for her boutique in Tehran. She was also an admirer of beautiful hand-made Persian rugs.

It was almost noon and I was still searching, desiring and awaiting the moment when a bolt of lightening would strike and I would be in love again. Eventually it did happen and we set aside three more rugs. My discipline of staying within budget and purchasing what I could afford all went out the big glass door behind where I was standing. I kept calm and reminded myself that bargaining the price of each rug would come later. I was just thrilled that the rugs had grabbed my attention. Mr. Asadi, however, did not want to talk price. He cheerfully announced that one could not think straight over empty stomach. He had ordered lunch, which was already awaiting us upstairs in his gallery. Mother and I, accompanied by Mrs. T, walked the narrow wrought-iron stairs that led to the upper section of the gallery—it was more like a mezzanine. Rugs and framed tapestries were everywhere, on the floor and on the walls. There was also lunch.

A low rectangular coffee table and several comfortable chairs were on one side. Newspapers were spread on the coffee table. A big platter of steaming saffron rice, skewers of savory golden chicken kabobs, grilled tomatoes, and several bottles of soft drinks were neatly arranged on the coffee table. The sight of the food was extremely appetizing, the aroma was tantalizing, and my stomach was shamelessly growling. I chuckled again. Mr. Asadi's customer service was impeccable. He was the consummate sales and marketing guru. I thought he could easily teach a thing or two at business schools, or at sales seminars. He broke bread with his customers and kept his word. Mother and several other close friends of my family have known Mr. Asadi for years. They never purchase rugs from anybody else but him. There is a mutual trust based on friendship and understanding.

It was almost two o'clock in the afternoon when we finished lunch, followed by another round of freshly brewed tea, along with a dish of hard candy loaded with cardamom seeds. While we were having lunch, Mr. Asadi had one of his office boys make copies of the pages of the book in which the history of the Pazyryk rug was described,

"Please give this to your daughter-in-law when she sees her rug." Mr. Asadi thought of everything.

Finally, the moment of truth arrived. We now had to talk price. It was rather peculiar that at that moment I remembered the famous line uttered by Ryan O'Neal in the last scene of the movie *Love Story*. I hoped I'll never have to say "I'm sorry" to my husband or to my daughter-in-law regarding my selections and the cost!

Mr. Asadi and his son positioned themselves on one side of his desk, Mother and I on the other side, facing each other with pens and tablets of paper in our hands. For each rug we recorded its dimensions, color, design, where it was made, the quality, and any other pertinent description and information. Then Mr. Asadi mentioned the price of each rug which I recorded. Mother and I did not show any indication of agreement or disagreement, joy, or disappointment. We simply recorded the facts. Like a poker player's face, we were void of any signs of emotion.

Then Mother and I went over the list and came up with our own prices, what we were willing to pay for each rug. We crossed out his prices and wrote down what we thought was the fair market value of each piece. Mr. Asadi looked at our numbers, consulted his son, and came back with a counter offer. We negotiated the price of each and every rug. When we finally reached a mutual agreement, Mohammad, who is also a business partner, began to write up the orders. Mrs. T, a silent observer of the entire negotiating process, got up at this point and bid us farewell and left the gallery.

But before she left, she whispered in my ear a complimentary comment on my selections. I was happy that my purchases were sanctioned by an expert, neutral third party. Mother was pleased with the prices she had negotiated, and Mr. Asadi thanked us for our business. It was precisely five o'clock in the afternoon when we left Mr. Asadi's rug gallery. By then I truly understood why my mother was so anxious to get an early start.

46

A Full Day

Tehran, Iran's capital city, has a reported population of close to nine million—or by some accounts around fifteen million considering the larger metropolitan area—with incredibly congested traffic and rampant air pollution. It is nearly impossible to accomplish more than one task per day. It is not just my opinion—friends who come from the United States to visit family in Tehran have the same view.

Today appears to be an exception. My mother is determined to get all her shopping done in one day. First she wants to visit a special bookstore and buy postcards depicting Persepolis and the mosques of Isfahan— these are for her son-in-law in New York. Then she wants to purchase pistachio nuts and dried fruits that I will bring back with me to the United States for family members.

We leave the house before nine o'clock in the morning and get into a cab. Since I don't know where we are going, I wait for Mother to give the address to the cabbie. But my mother has this peculiar habit of never knowing the actual street address of any place she goes—she knows the locations by sight and name—and that sometimes drives me crazy!

The cab driver mentions the names of several well-known streets. Upon hearing one particular name, she nods, "Oh yes, that is the one."

"But Ma'am I cannot go there," the cabbie announces politely.

"Why not?" I inquire.

"It is government regulation; only vehicles with special permit can enter that street. I don't have the permit, and if I break the rule, I'll have to pay a hefty fine," he explains.

Mother is determined to shop today, so we go to Plan B. "Fine, then head north and go to Tavazo," she tells the driver.

He knows where Tavazo is located, turns around and we are on our way.

Tavazo is a well-known store. They have excellent quality nuts, dried fruits, spices, and traditional Persian sweets. They also charge an arm and a leg for their products. Customers can sample any product they wish while they are shopping. And if they don't, the sales people come around offering fistfuls of pistachios, dried figs, apricots, and peaches.

Mother has her list—in her head of course—and knows exactly what she wants to buy and for whom. I ask the cab driver to stick around because I know we will need his help, and it will be hard to find another cab quickly after we have shopped. He gives me his cell phone number to call when we are done shopping, and drives around to find a parking spot.

My mother spends more than $300 on just nuts and dried fruits. I sample yummy dried peaches stuffed with ground almond and cardamom, dried plums, and some pistachio nuts the sales lady offers me. Shopping is done and I call the driver.

He is lucky to have found a parking spot in front of the store. He helps me with the bags and puts them in the trunk and we head back home. What a blessing that he could wait for us—needless to say he charges for his time dearly! One mission accomplished.

It is past noon when we arrive home. Mother is exhausted and has to lie down. I get busy fixing lunch for us.

"I want to visit my ophthalmologist this afternoon," she announces.

The surgeon who removed her cataract does follow-up checking of his patients, by appointment, only twice a week in the afternoon. Today is one of those days. It seems we are about to break the cardinal rule of "one task per day" and possibly accomplish two! She phones the doctor's office. We are on our way by 3:30 p.m.

Dr. J. is a well-known ophthalmologist in Tehran. His office is located north of the city, at the foot of the mountains in Farmanieh, a posh suburb. Even with the heavy afternoon traffic, another cab driver manages to get us there by 4:30 p.m. His office is crowded with patients—he works with two other doctors who are cornea specialists, and they have three optometrists on location. This office buzzes with activity. Old, young, male, and female patients with various stages of eye problems fill the two large waiting rooms.

I become interested in the patients sitting in the waiting room, and start taking pictures with my ever-present camera—discreetly at first, but openly later. People don't seem to mind.

By the time Mother is done visiting Dr. J, it is past 7:30 p.m. She is super-tired and famished. Mother is also diabetic and I know she has to eat soon, before we head back, which will take another hour in a cab ride in heavy evening traffic.

"Is there a restaurant close by?" I ask the receptionist.

"Yes, there is a good one, four blocks away."

Of course we need to get another cab as Mother cannot walk the distance and, due to eye drops, she cannot see well either.

Wow, another mission accomplished today!

We enter Gharashi Restaurant. It is very clean and cozy with only one other customer. It appears to be a "take-out" place as well. The restaurant specializes in kabobs, and they also serve pizzas.

I walk toward the counter and see a clay oven in the back. I ask for one meal to share with Mother. The server, a man of about forty, smiles and says he knows exactly what to fix us. I let him.

First he brings us a freshly-baked thin, round, flat bread, along with a bowl of thick yogurt. We dip the warm bread into the bowl—it tastes heavenly! Then he brings us a platter of three skewers of different kabobs: chicken, beef, and lamb, with French fries and pickles on the side. We devour all the food—a fabulous meal at a restaurant we didn't know existed.

I talk to the server and learn the restaurant owner is an old movie actor. The photo of the actor—in his younger years—is framed and is on the wall. Shortly thereafter, the actor himself walks in. He is wearing a black shirt, black pants, and with hair dyed jet black—he doesn't look anything like his framed photo. I take out my camera.

"May I take a picture of you and my mother together?" I ask with a smile.

He grabs his photo off the wall, holds it in front of him, and poses with my mother for an interesting Kodak moment. I see the resemblance.

Before we leave, the server gives us another freshly baked flat bread to take home as a gift.

It is past 10 p.m. when we finally arrive at the house, exhausted. We don't even turn the kitchen light on. We brush our teeth and quickly hit the sack.

Unbeknownst to us, Sara, the neighbor, has not heard any noise from my mother's place all day. She calls the neighbor across the street who has not seen any lights in the kitchen either. They keep calling the house to no avail. By 9 p.m. they call Aunt Tooran across town, who doesn't know anything about our plans.

The next morning all hell breaks loose!

I'm having breakfast with Mother in the kitchen. From the open window, I hear the neighbor across the street calling my name—I invite her to come up. She tells us how worried she was not to have seen any lights in the kitchen. At that exact moment Sara knocks and enters the house, makes inquiry regarding our whereabouts the night before, and says she has called Mother's sister. While I'm making a full disclosure of yesterday's activities, and confessing that we ate out last night, the phone rings. It is Aunt Tooran who wants to know where we were the night before!

In the midst of all the confession and apologies for not informing the neighbors of our plans, the phone rings again. It is my husband calling from the United States. We speak in English.

"Honey, rest assured," I say with a chuckle. "In this huge city of nine million folks, there is not a chance that your wife could possibly have a clandestine affair. I'm being watched every second by many self-licensed Private Eyes!"

Frankly, I must admit it is refreshing and comforting to know Mother's neighbors are watchful and caring. They truly are concerned about her safety and well-being. It is their love and attention that gives me the relative peace of mind to let her stay in her own house.

Even when my mother develops dementia in her final years of life, the bank employees, the green grocer, the folks in the corner store where she shops daily, all watch over her. I'm forever grateful for the humanity displayed by her neighbors, and other folks in her neighborhood. I am blessed to encounter decent people during my frequent trips to Iran. God bless them and their families.

Yes, it takes a village, for both young and old.

EPILOGUE

In the spring of 2001 my father passed away. In his last will and testament he had named me his executor. I felt the responsibility of carrying out the terms of his will to the fullest. Two important instructions, as I recall, were his emphasis on keeping his wife's comfortable life style intact for as long as she lived. And second, if possible, to spend some of the inheritance on charities and helping needy folks, particularly students who needed money to continue their education. My father believed in learning and education.

My two sisters and I have followed those instructions. The trips I made back to Iran were for the purpose of making sure Mother was fine and also to take care of whatever tasks she wanted me to do.

A few years after his passing, at the request of my mother, I went back to help her clean up his study. We donated the collection of his books to the local library at Park Shafagh. Some of his writings and books went to the relatives who asked for them. Then I came across all the correspondence he had meticulously kept throughout the years. To my absolute amazement I found a collection of all the letters I had sent to my parents during my high school year in the United States. For me, that discovery was a gold mine! Those letters enabled me to look into the mind and thinking of a 17-year-old girl who left a sheltered life in Iran to come to America for the first time. Those letters are the basis for my second book, *A Year in Middle America*.

We are the sum of our DNA, upbringing, environment, and the values instilled in us. Looking back on my own life, I'm grateful for the lessons I've learned from the people around me. Even when I was disciplined as a child, I never doubted the love my parents had for me. I suppose, in a way, I'm also dedicating this memoir to my deceased parents and the family members who had a hand in raising me.

Challenges with raising children, dealing with aging parents, and rapid societal changes do not recognize geographical boundaries—they exist in every culture and every country. I'm appreciative of who I am, the values I've learned, and the good people with integrity I've met on this long journey we call "Life."

ACKNOWLEDGEMENTS

For the past ten years Connie Shoemaker, a good friend from Colorado, has been urging me to write down my stories. Thank you Connie for not giving up, and pushing me to do so.

A very special thank you to Lindsay McSweeney who edited this manuscript. Her enthusiasm to read the next story was an impetus for me to keep on writing. Thank you, Lindsay.

Throughout the years I have belonged to various writing groups, and attended memoir writing classes—I thank them all.

Thank you to John Prince for guiding me through the nuances and pitfalls of self-publishing.

I want to thank my husband, who likes my sense of humor and chuckles whenever I share a story or two with him. Thank you, love, for all your support.

And thanks to my relatives and friends who will read these—please know these stories are mine, from my perspective, and are the way I remember them.

MEET THE AUTHOR

Manijeh Badiozamani is a literary non-fiction writer. She writes mostly about her experiences growing up in Tehran, Iran, where she was born, but also writes about her travels back to Iran. She has lived in the United States for the last 50 years. Her stories have been published in magazines, anthologies, and on the internet.

She earned a Ph.D. from the University of Idaho in education and has taught educational psychology, writing, and composition at the college level. She previously worked at a financial and investment company. She has one son, and currently lives with her husband in Florida. This is her first collection of short stories.

Made in the USA
Lexington, KY
22 November 2019